DOUBLE DUTY

DUAL IDENTITY

Raised in an Alcoholic/Dysfunctional Family and

GAY — LESBIAN

by Claudia Black, M.S.W., Ph.D.

ISBN No.: 0-910223-14-9

1st Printing, June 1990.

MAC PUBLISHING
a division of CLAUDJA, inc.
5005 East 39th Avenue
Denver, CO 80207
(303) 331-0148 • Fax (303) 331-0212

To my contributors, a.k.a.
Adriennne, David, Kim, Jean and John

ACKNOWLEDGEMENTS

I would like to express my gratitude to all of the contributors who participated in this project. While only five life stories appear in the final book I am also greatly indebted to the others who offered stories. These people displayed not only a rare courage and generosity — they reached deeply into themselves and discovered yet another level of their own recovery.

I would also like to acknowledge my professional friends who gave me feedback on various chapters throughout this series. Leslie Drozd, Ph.D.; Victoria Danzig, M.S.W.; Don Steckdaub, M.A.; Doug Braun, M.F.C.; Jill Borman; Jael Greenleaf; Ed Ellis, Ph.D.; Dana Finnegan; Emily McNally; Mel Pohl, M.D.; Skip Sauvain, M.A.; Wynn Bloch, M.A.; Wayne Smith; Betty La Porte and Sam Ryan.

Thanks to Mary McClellan, of San Francisco who worked with me on the presentation of those stories; Barbara Shor, for her copy editing. Anne Marsin for her typing and retyping that was so vital in this project; Cheryl Woodruff, the Ballantine editor of the book Double Duty, Jack Fahey, my husband and business partner who has read and reread every version of every chapter. He one more time walked me through this process every inch of the way.

CONTENTS

DOUBLE DUTY

While there has been a proliferation of books about Young and Adult Children of Alcoholics it is important to recognize that the Children of Alcoholics movement is still in its infancy. We are only now beginning to understand the complexity of the trauma within the dysfunctional family systems so many Adult children have experienced and the ways this has compromised their adulthood.

Over the past few years thousands of Adult Children have begun their process of self-healing. There have been many wonderful miracles. Yet, as I watched people moving through their recovery, I have also seen many individuals hit a baffling impenetrable wall that halted their progress. There seemed to be a missing link or another piece to the puzzle. A very big piece of what I believe causes such blockage is the experience that I call **Double Duty.**

I define **Double Duty** as the intensified life experiences of ACOAs who have contended, not only with family alcoholism or dysfunction, but have also dealt with an additional set of circumstances that have profoundly affected their lives and their recovery. Many Adult Children belittle and criticize themselves for not moving through recovery as easily or as speedily as others they know. When ACOAs are unable to work through the recovery process with as much ease or speed as they would like, it is often because of their need to identify and address multiple issues in recovery. People who have multiple issues often have an additional need to protect themselves, and this may be why they do not connect with self-help groups or the therapy process as quickly as others.

One of the key premises of the ACOA recovery process is putting the past behind us. That only occurs when the truth of one's experience is acknowledged. Up to this time in the evolution of the ACOA movement, the stories told — and as a result the issues addressed — have tended to be very generalized. This stage of emphasizing the experiences all ACOAs have in common has been incredibly valuable.

However, now that many Adult Children have spent several years in recovery from their ACOA issues, I believe it is time to explore how Adult Children differ from each other. This book describes in detail the process the child experiences in an alcoholic family. It also examines the special problems of multiple issues — which I call **"Double Duty/Dual Identity"** (DD/DI) — that these Adult Children face and the step-by-step process of their recovery. We can no longer continue to apply generic recovery programs to all ACOAs. While general recovery information is most often what one needs to focus on in early recovery, in time an individual's unique life situation has to be and deserves to be addressed. By refusing to look at the specifics of an individual's experiences we can inadvertently trivialize the purpose of the entire movement.

The concept of **Double Duty** is not meant to encourage people to use their differentness to keep others away or to resist new opportunities. I believe we must first see our commonalities, and humble and comfort ourselves in the recognition that we are not unique. Although, we suffered separately, we have not suffered alone. Only after we have acknowledged this common ground should we undertake to explore what may have been unique in our experiences.

There are many reasons for differences among Adult Children. Birth order affects children differently, sex role expectations affect children differently. Who the chemically dependent parent is and the dynamics of how co-dependency shows itself create differences among ACOAs. Many areas merit exploration, but I have chosen certain areas that warrant deeper exploration for the Adult Child in the recovery process. Double duty exists when a child has one major trauma-inducing dynamic in the family and there exists an additional dynamic that reinforces the consequences through added trauma or complexity.

For instance, if there is a terminally ill sibling in a child's family, growing up can be quite traumatic. But is does not have to create a lifelong trauma if there is a healthy family system to help the surviving child respond to the situation. However, put the set of circumstances in an alcoholic or otherwise troubled family, and the child involved will suffer many long-lasting effects from both issues. This is what I mean by a double duty situation.

In order to endure such trauma and added complexity — simply in order to survive — this child has to toughen up much more than other children. In adulthood, such survivors are likely to have their defenses much more rigidly in place and their emotions very hardened.

I envision the double duty COA as a small child, hunched over, dragging unwieldy boxes and overflowing bags of trauma, when suddenly a dump truck comes roaring up and adds another load of pain.

By contrast, **Dual Identity** is a special form of **Double Duty** in which one has at least two equally commanding aspects to one's identity — such as being a COA and a person of color or being a COA and gay or lesbian. It is like looking into a two-sided mirror and seeing one image of yourself on one side and an equally real but different image on the other side. Although the images are different, they are invisibly enmeshed. This leaves Adult Children even more confused about who they are and what is most important in their lives.

For the purpose of Adult Child recovery it is important to recognize that as an ACOA, there may be other, equally significant aspects of your identity that need to be recognized and addressed — beyond those of having been raised in a chemically dependent family — in order to experience a full recovery.

Double Duty/Dual Identity are examples of the synergistic effect of multiple-core issues that many Adult Children experience. The added dynamics of **Double Duty/Dual Identity** often force children to protect themselves even further. As a result, issues such as not trusting, not feeling, fear of losing control, and an overwhelming sense of shame are experienced even more deeply. It then becomes much more difficult for the afflicted ACOA to ask for help or to feel any hope. Very often the feeling of being overwhelmed by emotion or of having frozen emotions greatly impedes the ability to connect with a recovery process.

There are many people who know they are Adult Children, who know resources are available, who may even truly want to change their lives — yet always find that something seems to get in the way when they try to connect with a helping resource or try to stay involved once they've found that resource. There are others who are so powerfully defended against their pain that their level of denial is too strong for them even to recognize that their lives could be better. Still others become stuck in the process of recovery and "spin their wheels." These are often the DD/DI people. In this book we will explore the phenomena of being raised in an alcoholic/dysfunctional family and being gay or lesbian.

"Fear was what I knew growing up. I was afraid of coming home, being home, of leaving home, of being away from home, even of being at home. I didn't want to be whoever I was or wherever I was."

A Gay ACOA

GAY OR LESBIAN — DUAL IDENTITY

"Dual identity," a special form of double duty, means experiencing two identities simultaneously. In this case it is being both an Adult Child of Alcoholics and gay or lesbian as well. Dual identity often magnifies one's Adult Child issues. Because so many people are fearful and prejudicial toward homosexuality, gays and lesbians often face a constant struggle to feel good about themselves. Experiencing the homophobia so prevalent in our society, whether covert or overt, becomes a way of life.

When still quite young, many gays and lesbians learn to both deny and hide important aspects of the self from themselves and others. This leads to confusion and difficulty in trusting their own feelings and perceptions. They may find it difficult to trust others and to live with others' judgment, rejections, or punishment. They learn that to survive—to avoid being verbally, emotionally, and possibly even physically abused—a part of them must remain invisible. This continual discounting of self makes it difficult for them to feel good about who they are. As a result they segregate or fragment parts of their selves and their lives. Unfortunately this often results in isolation.

While homosexual children may have had to deny who they are in terms of their sexuality, children in the alcoholic family have had to deny their feelings and experiences of living in a strongly dysfunctional family. The tendency is to ignore one or the other of these issues, not recognizing how the combined dynamics of being both an Adult Child and homosexual reinforce each other. This book is about validating these experiences and how the dynamics of being lesbian or gay in an alcoholic family is a profound example of the *"double duty"* syndrome.

Growing up in an alcoholic family is difficult all by itself. Growing up gay or lesbian in an alcoholic home creates an environment in which children have an even greater need to defend and protect themselves from being hurt.

Although homosexuality and chemical dependency are different phenomena, COAs and gay and lesbian children often respond to their cumulative life stresses similarly. Loneliness, fear, isolation, denial, shame, being secretive, and not feeling good about oneself are already common issues for many gays and lesbians. Unless they were raised in an atmosphere that encourages them to develop high self-esteem, society's homophobia has made it necessary for gays and lesbians to adopt many Adult Child strategies. Both have to respond to an environment that does not feel safe: on the one hand the threat is posed by the community, on the other by the family. This leaves very little room to hide.

As young children they internalized terribly hurtful messages:

• You are different.

• You should be ashamed of what you do and therefore ashamed of who you are.

• It is not okay to be who you are.

• You can't trust your perceptions.

• You mustn't talk about what is occurring.

These unspoken messages create a life of guilt and shame—a life ruled by secrets and denial. With that denial comes incredible fear, loneliness, isolation and self-loathing. Unfortunately, too often neither gays and lesbians nor COAs experience any sense of belonging. Yet the sense of belonging, of feeling connected with others, is vital to a child's development and sense of self-worth. Growing up, many gays and lesbians have a sense that they are different, and they wonder why.

Not every gay or lesbian will identify with these issues, nor has every gay or lesbian had these experiences, but these experiences are very common themes for the gay and lesbian Adult Child.

LIFE STORIES

The following life stories are from five gays and lesbians, ranging in age from twenty eight to forty two, who were raised in chemically dependent families. During adolescence, all but one recognized that their sexual orientation was different from that of their peers. But for all of them the struggle around *"coming out"* publicly as gay or lesbian was relatively brief. They all accepted their sexuality at a young age. Clearly, being children in alcoholic families was much more traumatic than being homosexual in a heterosexual society.

Although we will discuss a number of issues, we will explore in depth the intensified dynamics of secrets and denial, guilt and shame, coming out, and Adult Child recovery considerations.

Please keep in mind that although the following stories are about people raised in chemically dependent families. It is not my contention or theory that being raised in a dysfunctional family creates homosexuality. There are a multitude of theories regarding homosexuality, ranging from physiological to psychological frameworks. These are gay and lesbian children who happen to live in disturbed families. In a few of these stories, you will see how a child may feel greater safety with the parent of one sex as opposed to another. And you'll be able to trace how such limited interactions may strongly influence later friendships and even shape the coming-out process. Nevertheless, being raised in an alcoholic/dysfunctional family is not cited as a cause of homosexuality.

GROWING—UP YEARS

ADRIENNE
Age: 33
Mother: Alcoholic
Father: Alcoholic
Stepfather: Alcoholic
Birth Order: Youngest of four
Raised: Midwest
Socioeconomic Status: Working class

Born into a family of two alcoholics, Adrienne was conceived as the result of one of her mother's extramarital affairs. She says that both her mother and her mother's husband were alcoholics for as long as she can remember, as were most of the people they associated with.

ADRIENNE:

"I felt guilt for being alive. I was told that kids were to be seen and not heard, and I got the distinct impression that they were a hassle to have around. This, in addition to fear, shame, and isolation, dictated how I felt about myself as a child, as a young woman, and as a lesbian."

When Adrienne was three her mother married Ed, her third husband. He was a violent, abusive man who constantly criticized and threatened Adrienne and her three older siblings.

"I would cower in bed listening to my parents fight and waiting for it to escalate to physical violence. At this point I would calmly walk out, sit down, and watch him.

"My mother told me that Ed would be less likely to hit her with me around — so I understood it was up to me to save her. When I was nine and doing 'guard duty' during one of these episodes, Ed put a

gun to my head and threatened to kill me and my mother. I remember sitting there smirking, and thinking, F——you.

"I hated my stepfather. My allegiance was to my mother, who I literally saw as my lifeline and comrade. Together, we would scheme how to deal with him, how to negotiate around his moods. I prided myself on being 'the best at handling him' of all the siblings and at being considered very grown-up for my age. I felt repeatedly devastated and betrayed when my mother would take him back after he'd beaten her or my brother. We owned two houses side by side — one supposedly for guests, but which was used more frequently as Ed's 'doghouse.' He had to stay there as punishment for beating up my mother or threatening us all. Whenever this happened, the local police would be called, and they would sit patiently in the driveway waiting for the whole thing to calm down."

Adrienne was caught in a web of confusion. She vacillated between feeling like her mother's confidant and protector and feeling abandoned. This is because, when Adrienne's stepfather wasn't available, her mother relied on Adrienne's strength and ability to cope. But when the stepfather was available, her mother relegated Adrienne to the role of neglected child.

"Growing up, I felt I was never quite good enough. But I also felt I should know how to do everything perfectly without any explanations. It was unsafe to ask questions, since my stepfather might call me stupid or scoff at my not knowing. I learned to fake things quite early. I faked being courageous, tough, and self-sufficient when I was actually very needy and scared. I faked knowing how to do something when I was confused and frightened, so that my ignorance would not be revealed. I faked being together and unaffected by criticism and humiliating comments, when I was really emotionally devastated."

"Never feeling good enough" is a common consequence of the stresses experienced by COAs, and Adrienne gained a lot of practice at this long before she would even know that her sexual identity would be added to the list of her inadequacies.

"School was always just sort of an okay place to be. I was an above average student as a way to get approval from teachers. I wanted to be liked. Fortunately, one teacher gave me a lot of encouragement with my writing, and that helped me aspire toward college.

"But I was most influenced by my family. My stepfather was extremely sexist and bigoted, — a mean version of Archie Bunker. I got the message at an early age that it was bad to be female and therefore horrendous to be lesbian. He believed that women were stupid and inept and, in fact, my mother seemed basically weak and powerless around him. She worked as an uncredited partner in their various businesses, smoothing over his rough relationships with people—but all he did was criticize her constantly. I got the idea that men were a hassle, like having another child to take care of. They had to be humored and manipulated."

Adrienne's siblings were considerably older than she, a sister and brother fifteen and thirteen years older and another brother seven years older. Adrienne felt closest to the older brother. She describes him as the family hero and remembers looking to him as a father at times. She remembers him as the only gentle man in her life. But Adrienne did as so many COAs do. She sought refuge outside the home.

"I spent as much time as possible away from home. Happy childhood memories are mostly of times I spent at my grandmother's home or at the home of my baby-sitter, who was a grandmotherly sort of person. My own grandma moved away when I was six, but she returned when I was eleven. I always had this feeling that I didn't quite belong at home, that home wasn't safe. For most of my young adulthood I continued to act this out, not really settling into places where I supposedly lived, and letting myself be 'adopted' by established couples.

"When I got involved in my first major, healthy relationship four year ago, I continued to sleep on friends' couches at least once a week during the first months of living with my lover because I simply didn't feel safe where I lived.

"As I became aware of my sexual and romantic feelings for women, it never occurred to me to consider telling anyone. My first crush was on my high school teacher, and by eleven I was crazy about my best friend. I was sure that I was the only one who was falling in love with and sexually fantasizing about her girlfriends.

"To figure out what was 'wrong' with me I read Everything You Always Wanted to know About Sex, which I read as saying basically homosexuality is a sickness. I believed this and clung to the author's assertion that adolescents might have homosexual feelings until they turned fifteen or sixteen, after which they would (hopefully) become normal. I was crushed when I turned sixteen and was still sexually and emotionally attracted to my girlfriends, my brother's wife, and my teachers. I felt that my lesbianism was literally a curse, and I was later shocked to discover that some women actually chose to become lesbians."

At such a young age, Adrienne internalized that she was wrong for loving girls. Already having learned that it wasn't safe to talk about her feelings and ask questions openly, she refused to squelch her feelings totally but secretly sought information through reading. However, she would find that all the literature classified homosexuality as a sickness, a malady of the mind. Having received no validation for homosexuality as a natural way being wherein she could find acceptance for herself in the world, she secretly hoped her feelings would change.

At the time Adrienne graduated from high school she was actively involved in what she called *"street fundamentalist Christianity."* She was enrolled in a religious college, but her stepfather was not willing to financially support her there, so she enrolled in a state college. Over the next few years she struggled with her sexual identity, assuming that the right person could help her become straight. However, by the time Adrienne graduated from college she had come to accept her lesbianism.

JOHN
Age: 28
Mother: Co-dependent
Father: Alcoholic
Additional: Parents recovering today
Birth Order: Youngest of six
Raised: Southeast
Socioeconomic Status: Upper middle class

The youngest of five children, John grew up with a father who was an alcoholic and a mother who spent a good part of his youngest years in and out of hospitals. (Some of the hospitalizations were for medical reasons, others were stress-related.) John himself was often very sick as a child. He had an operation when he was six for an inherited upper-respiratory disease and several eye operations as well. John's father was a builder, his mother a housewife.

John's mother was hospitalized for the first time when he was four. He describes those times as confusing and frightening.

JOHN:

"We would get notes from her. But I was always protected from all information. No one would explain to me why she was in the hospital. I don't know if my brothers and sisters were kept as protected as I was. At some point I was told she had tumors in her head.

"What I remember so clearly about my younger years was that I used to lie down on the floor next to the vent that led to my parents' bathroom and I would hear my mother crying all the time. She would go and hide in the bathroom and just sob for hours. This happened every night. Dad would be asleep on the couch, and Mom would have done all the dishes. Then she would go upstairs and cry. I would lie there, listening to her, because I knew it was as close as I could get to her. She would go to church all the time, and I could not imagine why

this God she worshipped would put her through so much pain and agony."

During his growing-up years, John related much more to his siblings and mother.

"My father was the provider. It was as if he was this person who was 'out there.' He was away from the house a lot. When he was home I remember most the unpredictability of his moods and how we were supposed to behave. The message was loud and clear. We were responsible for his moods. My strongest image of him was dozing on the couch. This was also the time we would ask him for things. He would murmer 'yes' just to get us out of there. I don't remember ever connecting any of what was occurring with alcohol and certainly not with alcoholism."

John's childhood relationships with his siblings were varied and typical of both a large family and an alcoholic family. He describes his relationship with his oldest brother as one of great rivalry and remembers they fought a lot. He saw this brother as the family foot soldier, the little adult trying to be in charge. John idolized his oldest sister and wanted to get closer to her, but it was as if she were always just out of reach. He saw her as someone safe yet far away from him.

He remembers that he and his middle sister were particularly close. She was his protector, his mediator, his mother, tucking him into bed each night. He says he and his youngest sister would always plan things to do together, but being close in age they were forever arguing.

John idolized his second oldest brother, Paul, who was also gay. During his teens John made many attempts to reach out to Paul, sensing that they might be able to talk about the sexual feelings John was having. But Paul seemed scared and avoided talking with John. How much of the *"Don't talk"* rule Paul was abiding by — due to the fear and shame of being gay or to the isolation of being in a chemically dependent home — is difficult to say. Most likely both played a role.

John attempted to deal with the family dynamics by taking on various roles at different times.

"I played every role there is in the alcoholic family: I adjusted; I was a placater; I was the responsible one; I was all of those things at different times. I acted out as well."

John was aware of his sexual attraction by the time he was nine.

"My first gay encounter was when I was in the fifth grade, and it continued with the same person until I was a junior in college. The 'Don't talk' rule was firmly intact. We never discussed what we were doing. From the beginning we used either alcohol or pot in order to be sexual. We started by taking shots from his dad's liquor cabinet, and that would make the sex okay. As the years of our interactions progressed, so did our use of chemicals. My adolescence was made up of fear, secrecy, and repression. Alcohol and other drugs were clearly an answer for me.

"My own addiction began when I was only twelve years old. Even when I was as young as six, I remember the buzz I would feel when I drank cough syrup. I used to love it! By the time I was twelve, alcohol had become a major form of escape."

John's own addiction precluded his having many clear memories of his family during his teenage years. In many ways he became a lost child, lost to alcohol, drugs, fear.

John's use of alcohol and drugs began at a young age, which is often true for COAs. Many begin to drink and use by the time they're eleven or twelve. John's use of pot and alcohol during sexual encounters is not unusual for either heterosexuals or homosexuals. In pre-adolescence and adolescence, sexual behavior is often synonymous with drinking and using.

John's fear of being caught and of making others ashamed of him were far more traumatic for him than his actual sexual behavior. Clearly he was being raised in a family so shrouded in secrets that no matter what his sexual behavior might be, it would have been performed behind a veil of secrecy. The fact that his behavior was homosexual simply multiplied his fears. Alcohol and drugs would become a temporary answer to both his fear and his secretive behavior.

KIM

Age: 33
Mother: Chemically Dependent
Father: Co-dependent
Birth Order: Third of four children
Raised: West Coast
Socioeconomic Status: Upper middle class

Kim grew up with well-educated, liberal, professional parents. When she was three her mother was hospitalized for the first time with a *"breakdown"* — and this led to abuse of tranquilizers and alcohol.

Kim says she remembers being given a lot of attention in her first three years.

KIM:

"And I spent the next twenty years trying to recapture that time. My mother was the type of person who drank in isolation. She would go to her bedroom and lock the door for hours — even days.

Kim also remembers that her mother had good times as well as bad. But Kim had a sister who was severely depressed.

"My mother saved her good times for my sister."

Kim spent her growing-up years by being the *"junior mom"* in the family.

"I was responsible and a hard worker, I got good grades in school and took care of my depressed sister. Through my adolescence I continued doing many mother-type things. My oldest brother escaped early be getting the most healthy family time. Then he left for college. My next brother was an angry scapegoat, always in trouble and being punished; I was the family caretaker and responsible child. My sister internalized everything and became progressively more depressed. She committed suicide at eighteen.

"My focus of concern was the family. I was the only child who really named the elephant in the living room. I pointed out to my parents repeatedly and loudly that they had problems. Finally, one night at the dinner table when I was sixteen, I announced flat out that my mom had a drinking problem. It was denied. It was then I started trying to figure out how I could leave—and if that would be deserting my sister.

"I took my mother's inaccessibility very personally. I went around looking for nurturing, and got a lot of it from the mothers of my girlfriends, particularly my best friend's mother. Female teachers were also very important. My girlfriends were very important. What I felt as a teen was that if anything happened to any of my close friends, I would die. When my best friend would be gone for two weeks every year on a family vacation, I'd be almost non-functional with worry. She, and her family, were like emotional life rafts to me."

Kim's ability to depend on her friends for emotional support was one of her strengths. This response to her unhappy home life was not driven by her sexuality — it was the reaction of a young COA seeking friendship and validation.

Aside from *"one moment"* during her teens, Kim was not aware of feeling sexually attracted to women until she was in her twenties. The one moment took place one night when she was fifteen. A girlfriend was spending the night. While they were sleeping in separate beds in the middle of the night, their arms touched.

"It didn't feel sexual, but I know there was something different. It was not just a casual touch. But I didn't spend any time thinking about it. I had boyfriends. But although the time I spent with boyfriends was pleasant enough, looking back, I'm aware that it was as if I was waiting for something more. Boyfriends were just a ho-hum experience."

Kim felt a strong bond with the women in her life but would come to experience great loss in her relationships with all three women in her immediate family.

"Through my youth, three females in my family were most important to me — my mother, my sister, and my aunt. But by my mid-teens, my mother's disease was progressing, my sister was going nuts, and my aunt had moved across the country."

The loss Kim experienced in her relationships with significant males in her life was not as strong as the loss she felt with the three women. Kim never had the opportunity to develop a strong initial male bond.

"There were three men in my life at the same time, but for whatever reasons, they were not as important to me emotionally. I blamed my father for my mother's inaccessibility, because he was often the gatekeeper between her and myself. He was preoccupied with work, my mom, and their traveling. My parents had invested wisely and often traveled abroad. I remember clearly being told, 'We need some time away from you kids.' I idolized my oldest brother, but he wasn't around very much. And my parents set up my older brother and me as rivals. Although I was younger, they perceived me as the most capable and gave me more responsibility, which my brother greatly resented."

DAVID

Age: 32
Mother: Co-dependent
Father: Alcoholic, violent
Birth Order: Youngest of three
Raised: Northwest
Socioeconomic Status: Working class

David grew up with an alcoholic father who was constantly depressed and suicidal. He describes his family life as a mixture of his father's violence and his mother's pleas for the violence to stop. The parents were so focused on each other that they basically neglected and ignored their three children.

DAVID:

"They never had time for us. We were three little parents at a very young age. I liked playing house with my sister. At first glance my family looked very nonsexist, allowing their little boy to dress in girls' clothing and play 'housewife.' But in reality our parents had little interest in the differences among us. We were simply 'the children,' and as such we were kept sheltered as much as possible from the insanity that surrounded us. My mom would try to shelter us by directing Dad's attention away from us — keeping us on a separate floor from Dad or trying to calm him down in front of us. Or we were used in little ploys to keep my father from doing something crazy, like leaving my mother or killing himself. I do not remember one day when my father was not drunk.

"My house was predictably unpredictable. After a while, the nightmarishness became commonplace, and my father's self-involved, depressive, suicidal behavior was the expected norm. But I never got over the anxiety; neither did my brother and sister. We didn't talk about it much, though. I remember once declaring to them that I didn't believe in God, because He did not stop my daddy from drinking. The unfairness of the world hit me at a young age. I was incredibly angry."

David felt despised by his father. He felt he was never *"good enough"* for his father, that there was something wrong with him.

"We never talked. We never got along. As time went on, it didn't matter what my father wanted, and it didn't matter what I did — he was always dissatisfied. I felt singled out by him. It was not that he saw me as unique, but rather that somehow I touched a primitive sort of nerve in him, and he despised me.

"He would drink and cry, and tell me that he loved me. But then he'd let the neighbors' kids ride the tractor on our farm — a pleasure that my younger brother and I were denied because we 'might get hurt.' Of course my sister wasn't allowed to do these things, either — she was a girl, and he didn't like girls much. Although a drunk, my

father was an incredibly perceptive man. It may have been the part of me that was feminine rather than effeminate that he so disliked."

When David reached puberty he realized that he was *"different"* from his friends. He tried to alter his behavior in order to fit in.

"As I approached puberty, I awaited the time when, like my friends, I would start to look at girls' breasts and be interested enough to make lewd bathroom comments. Instead, I learned to be quite a little actor. I would talk about the female physique with as much fervor as my friends, but I felt like a fake.

"I began to read books about sex. I was aware that I was attracted to some of the male teachers and to some of the boys in high school, and I was terrified. I began to feel the same sense of loss that I felt about my family. I had never experienced the kind of family that television depicted on My Three Sons and Father Knows Best. Now I was cheated again because I saw my friends experiencing something I was not able to — adolescence."

David desperately needed to feel validation for being who he was. He wasn't asking for a lot — simply to have a basic childhood need met. But by adolescence he knew his validation would never come from his father. Yet when the time came that he knew he shoud be able to get it from his friends, his lack of sexual interest in girls made him feel that his own body and heart had betrayed him. Once more he was to find that he was perceived as different in a way that was not acceptable.

"So I escaped into fantasy. I became obsessed with rock-and-roll singers and dreamed of living in faraway places. I drew, and I wrote poetry. And I denied every feeling.

"I also escaped into mystical books. The writings of Kahlil Gibran seemed to be a source of purity — they gave me a sense of peace. I was continually torn between my desire for security, sunlight, and joy — and the cloud-like darkness that overshadowed my home.

"Being gay, even though I was fighting it, was just one more struggle I had to go through. Once again I couldn't live normally. All

I'd ever wanted was to live and feel normal. I wanted to have happy parents who were nice to each other and the kids. I wanted a father I could talk to. And now I didn't even feel a part of my friends. I couldn't join in the conversation because I wasn't interested in girls and I wasn't athletic.

"There was a double loss — the loss of family image and family life and the loss of friendships and peers. And then came a third major loss. Everything I was reading about gay men told me they were effeminate and listened to disco music. Once again I didn't fit in. I was a hiker and a gardener. I listened to Crosby, Stills and Nash. I didn't even fit into what I thought the gay world was!"

JEAN

Age: 42
Mother: Co-dependent
Father: Alcoholic
Birth Order: Oldest of two
Raised: South
Socioeconomic Status: Middle class

Jean grew up with an alcoholic father whose rages made family life frightening and miserable. Jean's mother was very co-dependent and constantly catered to or excused her husband's behavior.

JEAN:

"Even before my father had begun to drink a lot, he was volatile and very angry. He had a raging temper, with no patience or tolerance for anything. He would misplace his tools and then blame my brother or me. He would yell if he got frustrated trying to do a project around the house. He would yell at my mother for forgetting to put milk on the table for his coffee, even though she waited on him hand and foot. He would yell about the neighbors, about his co-workers, or his boss

— but he would never confront them directly. I was afraid of my dad. The drinking just made it worse. I would do anything to stay out of his way."

By the time Jean was nine, her father's drinking has increased significantly. At the same time, her mother began to work outside the home.

"We never talked about what was really going on. We pretended that our family life was happy. But it was violent with a lot of yelling and drinking. We never knew when dad would be home or how bad he would be when he arrived.

"I remember one Christmas Eve when we were getting ready to go to my grandmother's house to celebrate with the family. My father was raging drunk and threw all of my mother's clothes out the door into the snow. There was screaming and tears. But when we got to my grandmother's, Mother made excuses for my dad not being with us, saying he wasn't feeling well. And she reminded my brother and me not to tell what had really happened. Christmases were filled with fights and drinking. They were filled with fear and faking it — pretending that everything was wonderful. Faking it was the only way to survive."

Sadly, Jean's life was typical of many COAs, ridden with chronic fear. She was clearly afraid of her father's behavior whenever he was around and terrified of what he might do in the future. Jean's emotional survival was based on suppressing these fears and pretending that life was wonderful. That fear increased her need to deny. And before long she was going to have to learn that it was necessary to deny her *"differentness"* as well.

"I felt different in the first place because my dad yelled and got drunk and because I couldn't talk with anyone about it. But I also felt different because I was a tomboy and always wanted to do things that boys were allowed to do, like play baseball and football, climb trees, and play with trucks. I also felt different toward other girls. And I knew

I felt different. I would feel protective, like I knew guys were supposed to feel about girls."

Jean's first crush was on a camp counselor when she was eight years old.

"She was not particularly attractive, but she was warm, gentle, and loving. I felt safe with her, and I felt strong with her. I could forget all the battles and the drunken rages of home when I was away in a safe place like camp."

Jean felt awkward about feeling attracted toward her female friends or teachers and kept her feelings secret from her friends. When she was sixteen she began dating boys.

"I was attractive and popular, so I dated frequently. I usually went out with two or three guys at the same time, never going steady with one particular boy. They were nice, boys my mother would approve of."

It was also at this time that her mother learned to drive, bought a car, and moved Jean and her brother out of the house.

"It was a secret move, while my dad was at work. My mother took only the bare essentials because she didn't want to leave my dad with nothing. We moved because my dad's drinking and raging were getting worse. We were gone for only a few months, but I remember this as a very calm and peaceful time.

"I had been my mother's confidant since I was twelve, and now I was my mother's counselor as well. I listened without sharing any of my own feelings. My role was to be there for my mother. It made me feel very adult. I loved it because it gave me a connection with my mother.

"But then my parents reconciled, and we moved back home. My dad learned to control his temper, and my mother learned how not to provoke a fight. We spent the next couple of years walking on eggshells.

"*Although I still had this sense of being different, by the time I was in high school I was fitting in more. I was in the band, I was in honors classes, and I was college-directed. My mother's father wouldn't send her to college because he said it was no place for women. But my mother had always encouraged me to get a college education. Surprisingly, my father was also proud of my academic achievements and supported my going to college. I graduated from high school at seventeen and moved out of that environment when I entered college in the fall.*"

Irrespective of the fact that Adrienne, John, Kim, David, and Jean are gay and lesbian, they were children brought up in families affected by chaos, unpredictability, and unrealistic expectations on the part of the parents. They lived with chronic fear and loneliness. Adrienne had to respond to chronic physical abuse. John was a chronically ill child whose father was absent a lot and a nonentity when home and whose mother was so emotionally distraught that she required hospitalization. Both Kim and John describe their parents as extremely inaccessible, clearly due to the chemical dependency and co-dependency. David was extremely anxious having to react to a very critical alcoholic father who fluctuated from suicidal depression to violence. Jean lived in chronic fear of the next argument or fight. Their struggle to feel "*good enough,*" "*adequate,*" and "*of value,*" will be significant as a result of their being Adult Children.

These are people who deserve a path to recovery for the losses and traumas of their childhood. Acceptance of themselves, including their homosexuality, is much more likely when ACOA issues are addressed.

SPECIAL ISSUES FOR THE GAY AND LESBIAN ACOAS

Secrets and Denial

Gay and lesbian Adult Children have spent their lives keeping secrets. Like other children in alcoholic homes, they have had to keep the secret of the alcoholism. But on top of this, gays and lesbians are burdened with the secret of their own sexual identities, finding it necessary to keep secrets from a family that is already laden with secrets. This results in the *"living the lie"* syndrome, in which the children have to deny both what the family is and who they are. They become adroit actors, keeping up the illusion of a heterosexual self as well. These secrets accentuate the fear and shame of being discovered.

For Adrienne, keeping secrets was an accepted, seemingly necessary, and at times and even enjoyable part of everyday life in her family.

ADRIENNE:

"When I was young I was puzzled by the thought that in court people were expected to 'tell the truth, the whole truth, and nothing but the truth' just because they had their hand on a Bible and were on a witness stand. It seemed ridiculous to think that someone would tell the truth when at best it would probably get them into trouble and at worst bring punishment and ridicule."

Adrienne remembers conspiring with her mother to keep secrets from her stepfather.

"I'd feel clever and passively victorious at 'putting one over' on him. When he called me stupid, in addition to feeling stupid and bad, I would also revel in the fact that I could successfully lie to and manipulate him. There was no positive payoff for being honest for honesty's sake, so I learned to omit information and to lie whenever it was necessary to protect myself. As a co-alcoholic, I also distorted and omitted information whenever I thought someone 'couldn't

handle' the real facts. I was also passive-aggressive and used sarcasm or the silent treatment to express anger.

"My friends were all ACOAs, so the violent, erratic behavior of male alcoholics seemed normal. I thought and acted as though people from nonalcoholic families were boring, I lied to myself, denying that my family was oppressive and abusive, that in fact I would have loved to trade in my family for an Ozzie and Harriet model."

It is very difficult for children raised in alcoholic families to say, *"I hurt," "I'm sad,"* or *"I'm afraid."* But it is doubly difficult and unsafe for gay and lesbian COAs to say those things. Children who feel hopeless, that life could never be different, learn to do as Adrienne did — they take pride in learning how to survive. For instance, Adrienne was proud of her ability to lie and manipulate. Such children feel strength in their anger, and they will scoff at what seems to them to be an impossible dream — a nonoppressive, a nonabusive family.

The secret-keeping skills that Adrienne learned in her chemically dependent family made it easier for her to keep her sexual feelings a secret, too.

"When my lesbianism began to emerge at the age of nine, I kept these feelings a secret. They just confirmed my sense of being guilty, defective, not good enough."

Being raised in such a abusive family environment, Adrienne had already strongly internalized a sense of shame. She was also hearing clear messages that to be homosexual was bad. So when she became aware of her physical attraction to girls, this added a new burden of shame.

John said he learned to keep secrets at a very young age.

JOHN:

"It was easy to do because nobody wanted to talk about anything that was going on. I spent most of my childhood afraid.

"I was fearful of being ostracized because I'd seen a neighbor do that to his gay son. I saw and heard teenagers pick on gay guys. As a

little kid I was already being picked on for that. I was constantly afraid of being beaten up. Their verbal threats and name calling really terrified me.

"I never told anybody, until I was seventeen, that I was gay because I was scared to death. I was not only afraid that others would find out about my being gay, but I was afraid that my family would be criticized for my gayness.

"I also didn't want to add to the family pain. We already had so many problems. One of my sisters was abusing chemicals, two sisters had eating disorders, and one brother was openly gay. And, of course, there were my alcoholic parents. I was so afraid of being a negative reflection on my parents."

It is ironic that John was still trying to uphold the family *"image"* when it was already riddled with stigmatic addictions. John's reactions to his family's dysfunction reflects the incredible strength of his denial and the desire to be a caretaker.

John's need to cover up his true feelings, his true identity, led him to do various things to convince other people he was okay, which to John meant not being identified as gay.

"Anyone who has ever tried to hide a secret knows the games we play with ourselves and others in order not to be found out. Overtly we change our expressions, our manners. We become accustomed to delivering desired responses, signals and messages. We alter our stories, abilities and pronouns. This game of trickery requires constant attention and energy, and we end up living a chronic and painful lie."

The denial that goes into maintaining the false image of normality plays a big part in the life of an alcoholic family. Although members of the family are often silent about the secret of family alcoholism, it is nevertheless a secret they all maintain together. Yet the gay or lesbian secret is an individual secret that creates even more isolation for the homosexual COA.

This need to deny and sense of faking it makes it very hard for gay and lesbian children to interact socially with other children their age. They often feel like outsiders when they're with their peers — outsiders twice over, first because of the secrets of their home life and second because of their sexuality.

JEAN:

"I felt different from the beginning. I always wanted to be a boy. Even when I was as old as fourteen or fifteen, I still wanted to do the things boys did. I didn't want to have to wear dresses — although I did, and people said I was pretty. I still felt different, even though most people thought I fit right in with our group in high school. I felt as though I was playing a role, faking it, being an actor.

"Faking it seems to be a good way to describe much of my growing up. I faked being a girl. I faked being a good student. I faked being comfortable around my classmates. One rule stood out: Never talk about what went on at home to the kids at school. It always made me feel as if they were better than I was."

KIM:

"I learned how to keep major parts of my life secret from others — sometimes even secret from parts of myself. So it was easier to keep my lesbianism a secret from my family, until my recovery from my Adult Child issues made the pressure of the secret too heavy. So, breaking the secret of my sexual orientation with my parents two years ago seemed to me to be intertwined with what I learned as both an untreated ACOA (don't share) and a treated one (share and let go of the consequences). Actually, it has turned out pretty well."

Adult Children will often do anything to avoid further rejection. One of their major sources of self-protection is denial. They use denial to discount their homosexuality as well as the pain of the alcoholic or chemically dependent family. Denial coupled with secrecy adds fuel to this sense of shame and escalates the inner conflict.

Shame And Guilt

Shame is a very strong emotion in children. Shame is the belief that there is something inherently wrong with who we are. When we're shame ridden, we believe we're inadequate, different, or bad. Simply put, guilt is when you make a mistake; shame is when you believe you are the mistake.

Children in alcoholic families live lives of shame and fear. They're afraid that someone will find out what their family is really like. They're afraid people will see the violence, the ugliness, of their lives. They're afraid of feeling exposed and publicly shamed. Out of shame, they also take on the burden of feeling personally responsible for the family's disease.

Children in alcoholic families also experience a great deal of guilt — the feeling of regret or responsibility about something they have done or have not done. But much of their guilt is false guilt; it is a sense of responsibility for other people's feelings and actions. True guilt is the feeling of remorse for one's own feelings and behavior. It implies that one had developed a sense of responsibility for one's personal actions and feelings.

The alcoholic family's message is: *"Don't talk about what's really happening. Don't talk about your feelings."* But for the gay or lesbian child, there is an added message: *"Hide your sexuality. You are not acceptable."* It is very, very difficult for such children to feel good about who they are. In a society that largely condemns the expression of sexual feelings between people of the same sex, children who are gay or lesbian are made to feel ashamed and guilty for being who they are.

Adrienne describes feeling chronically guilty and shamed much of her childhood and until she was several years into recovery.

ADRIENNE:

"Guilt is a still a knee-jerk reaction I have for many situations for which I am not responsible. I felt particularly guilty about having been

born in the first place — especially when I found that I wasn't planned and was borderline illegitimate (the consequence of an extramarital affair). I felt as though I'd wrecked my mother's life — that they could have had an easier life if I weren't around. My mother seemed to operate from guilt, and I learned it quite well. I felt guilty if I disappointed somebody, made them mad, or made waves of any kind.

"And I certainly felt shame about my sexual thoughts and attractions. My lesbianism felt like a curse. I was terrified — and I ate. As a child and teenager I was always about twenty pounds overweight. It was just enough so that I could be unattractive and guys wouldn't bother me much. It was a part of my way of dealing with my fears, my guilt and my shame for being who I was."

JEAN:

"The shame I experienced was first related to my family. I was ashamed of who we were and how we lived. The next piece of shame was related to my sexually addictive behavior in college, which was fueled by both my own homophobia and my alcoholism. My next wave of shame came after my college years when I got involved twice with married men. I felt shame because they were married and again because of the conflict of my feelings of attraction for women."

For Kim, as for Jean, there was greater shame in being part of a dysfunctional family than in being a lesbian.

KIM:

"Not being too aware of any lesbian feelings, there was no shame connected with my sexual identity. My shame — and I certainly felt shame — was based on Adult Child issues. I was most ashamed for having needs. My parents were away a lot, and I wanted them to be in my life more. Whether I felt this more than my siblings is hard for me to know, but I was clearly the only one who felt devastated when they were away.

"My needs were normal childhood needs. I wanted my parents involved in my life. What I remember most is that somehow I was bad for wanting attention. I was bad for having needs. Somehow by age *four I was supposed to be this totally autonomous creature. The words I felt about myself were 'dumb,' 'stupid,' and 'bad'. So I did the best I could to become that autonomous little person and not feel the pain associated with being abandoned."*

Adrienne masks her shame with anger and compulsive eating. Jean masks her shame with sexually addictive behavior and alcohol. Kim finds a less blatant defense: she becomes invisible. David becomes isolated. And John discovers alcohol and drugs. These are ways that anyone affected by shame could respond.

Others respond with depression, or perfectionism, or by getting involved in hurtful and destructive relationships. Compulsive spending and workaholism are other possibilities. The ultimate act of shame may be suicide. In such cases a person may be feeling *"I am worthless. I am hopeless. I do not deserve to live."*

The responses to shame vary, but consequences of shame are the same whether or not one's shame emanates from childhood disruption or homophobia. However, gay and lesbian adult children bear the weight of double duty shame and feel it even more intensely.

DAVID:

"The strongest feelings I had as a child were guilt and shame, first because I was gay. I honestly think I would have traded anything to be heterosexual in my adolescence. Not that my fantasies weren't pleasant — they were natural and comfortable — but the aftermath was torture. The second reason for my guilt and shame was my family environment. I was afraid my friends would find out who I really was and they would abandon me."

David describes his childhood as a cycle of fear, guilt, and shame; fear, guilt, and shame; fear, guilt, and shame.

"I always felt wrong about everything. Certainly my parents always told me I was wrong about everything. So when I had these other emotions — love, attraction, and sexual feelings that seemed so natural — I was confused and immediately felt wrong. I felt shameful, and incredibly guilty. In essence, I equated good, happy feelings with

being wrong. I can remember always being fearful of disapproval and rejection. By my teenage years I knew I wasn't going to get any approval from my parents, so my peers were my only chance. But once again I was different, and this was not acceptable. I had to disown myself to be accepted."

JOHN:

"I had a terrible sense of fear when I was growing up. It was the basis for so many emotions, actions, and motivations. I was afraid of coming home, of leaving home, of being away from home, even of being at home. I didn't want to be wherever I was. I felt guilty about practically everything.

"I saw the pressure and the anxiety that was provoked when my brother and other gays I was aware of came out. No one seemed to understand homosexuality. Everyone seemed to want to change it, to control it. It was just crazy. And I was scared. I was fearful that I might be gay. And if somebody found out — that just fueled my sense of living in fear and the sense of shame that went along with it. I felt trapped and I wanted to escape. I've always punished myself a lot. I think I did that with my own addiction. I put myself through hell — isolation, suicide attempts, self-hatred, shame, which led to outbursts of rage and resentment."

Both Adrienne and David had the experience of hearing clear messages about homosexuality being bad.

ADRIENNE:

"My negative feelings about being a lesbian were exacerbated by my stepfather's physical and verbal abuse not only of me, but also of my brother. Stan was seven years older and also gay. When I was eight I remember my stepfather getting drunk and chasing Stan around the house, threatening to kill him because he was 'a goddamn little faggot.' The message was loud and clear that being a homosexual could literally get you killed."

DAVID:

"Once my sister used the word queer in the house. I do not know when the shouting, the banging, and the threatening stopped. I was no more than eight or nine at the time. The next morning, I asked what the word meant and why my father had gotten so upset over a word. My mother told me that it meant 'men who play with each other.' I felt ashamed, and I declared to myself at that point that I was not 'one of them.' It was not what Daddy wanted.

"When my father used the term homosexual, or any variation of it, I was filled with shame and regret. The way he used that word forced me to stay in the closet. To prove him right would have meant an utter loss of self and independence. But I ended up losing my self anyway by staying in the closet."

Any parental condemnation about a child's sexual orientation is usually exacerbated by society's taboos. The child hears from school, from peers, and from the media that homosexuality is bad and immoral. If the child has also grown up exposed to religious beliefs that condemn homosexuality, the part of the recovery process that asks one to accept a Higher Power becomes very difficult.

DAVID:

"My parents' religious fervor succeeded in making me a guilt-ridden young man. I would pray to God to take away the 'cross' — and it was not my father's alcoholism I meant. I think I would have traded anything to be heterosexual. I, too, became very religious and safely tucked myself away from facing my sexuality."

JOHN:

"I felt as if the fighting in the family were all my fault, and that if I would just do what was right, then everyting would be okay. In my strict Catholic upbringing, the concept of sin and punishment was so strong that I lived in fear and perpetual guilt because it wasn't possible to be the saintly child they described.

"The two most important areas of my life were my family, which was being torn apart by alcoholism, and the Church, where I felt only

rigid condemnation. I was so confused about the Church. I can remember a particular Bible verse that says, 'If you are poor, I will feed you; if you are naked, I will clothe you.' Every time that was said I always pictured a naked man. I don't know what others pictured, but I know that was wrong, and that I was wrong for thinking it. I finally had to give up on the Church because I felt so guilty. All I know is that sex, which began when I was very young, had to be secretive and hidden."

"Coming Out"

Openly Proclaiming One's Sexual Identity

Spending one's childhood laden with fear, guilt and shame makes one extremely vulnerable. Living with a sense of differentness that has been discounted, denied, and held secret would understandably confuse and overwhelm any young person. All children need to be able to feel safe speaking the truth. They need to be able to talk honestly about their feelings and perceptions. They need to be able to trust that others will listen. Ultimately, to feel good about themselves, they need to unload the secrets, to be honest about how they're living their lives.

An important part of the recovery process for Adult Children is to talk honestly about one's childhood and adult feelings and experiences. It means sharing the secrets that have been shrouded with shame for so long. But the homosexual Adult Child has two major secrets: chemical dependency in the family and his/her sexual identity. These double duty issues reinforce the difficulty of acknowledging either one. But recovery means learning self-love and self-acceptance, and that requires painstaking honesty, with oneself and with others.

Although people are slowly coming to accept the struggles involved in growing up in an alcoholic family, most of society is still ready to condemn homosexuality as wrong. The long-internalized shame often adds to the complexity of the coming-out process. While Adult Children have learned that the *"Don't talk"* rule no longer applies to the subject of alcoholism, gays and lesbians can still pay a big price for talking openly about their sexuality.

Adrienne's coming-out process began in college. But first she had to overcome her stereotypes of homosexuals as seedy low-lives hanging out in bars. She had begun seeing a therapist in college, who told her to *"get off the fence"* and decide once and for all whether she was straight or lesbian.

ADRIENNE:

"After a tortuous process, I decided to give up fighting my feelings for women and declare myself 'bisexual.' That was much easier to accept than simply being a lesbian. I started hanging out in discos with gay men.

"Then I met Rosa. Rosa was a gorgeous, feminine, happy Chicano lesbian who befriended me and introduced me to other lesbian women. Rosa defied my stereotype of lesbians as ugly, miserable, short-haired, lecherous alcoholics puking in bars. For the first time I was able to see that lesbians could be bright, productive people. I was thrilled to be able to identify. I embraced this new community of friends, feeling that I had indeed come home."

In her fourth year of college, Adrienne moved off campus and began to be actively involved in the gay community. She became a lesbian separatist. She had come out.

For the first time Adrienne had a sense of belonging. For the first time she was feeling accepted for who she was. In becoming a separatist she was fully embracing herself. However, she had not yet recognized some very important issues that would interfere with her ability to truly love herself.

"Although coming out seemed the answer to my problems, I had a long way to go. My co-alcoholism was in full swing, and my relationships were either fleeting sexual flings or unrequited love with my best friends. I had a terrible body image and was intermittently bulimic. All of my friends were from dysfunctional families, and none of us knew about the ACOA phenomenon."

Although Adrienne had come out as a lesbian, it would be a while before she began to address her Adult Child issues. For Kim, the two were meshed.

KIM:

"My coming-out issues were intertwined with my co-dependency/ACOA issues. Although I had begun my first lesbian relationship when I was twenty one, neither I nor my lover had labeled ourselves

lesbian. We were 'good friends' who slept together. Living in denial was natural for me — it was all part of living life on autopilot."

Kim had been raised with a mentally ill sister whom she dearly loved and had always sought to protect. Kim's attachment to her sister was one of the most significant relationships in her life.

"My sister killed herself when I was in this lesbian relationship. I was devastated — totally overwhelmed emotionally. I went into a major numbing period for four years, putting most of my grief issues on hold, and certainly the lesbian issues. I was nonsexual for those four years."

Few COAs can grieve for such a loss because they never learned to feel the "lesser" feelings, let alone the deepest of all. The sadness, the powerlessness, the guilt, and the rage that Kim felt had no safe avenues for expression. Numbing herself totally was what she had to do simply to keep walking through life.

"I worked eighteen hours a day at meaningless jobs and eventually went to graduate school. It wasn't until 1983 — four years after the death, five years into the relationship — that I began to think of myself as lesbian."

It is nearly impossible to address your sexual identity when you are in total denial. It is impossible to address your sexual identity when you are frightened of dealing with any aspect of your life.

KIM:

"Although when I was a teen I'd labeled my mother an alcoholic, somewhere along the way I got back into denial. There was a lot of stuff around protecting my parents after my sister's death, so I was in denial about everything — my mother's alcoholism, the reality that my sister had killed herself, and my own life-style.

"As a result of being suicidally depressed, I sought therapy and was fortunate in finding a wonderful therapist. She guided my gently through the morass, and in time I came to terms with it all. I was able to grieve for my sister, myself, the end of the five-year relationship, and everything else that needed to be grieved for.

"Until I came out as an ACOA, I could not come out as a lesbian. I think my emotional connection with women is very much part of growing up with an alcoholic mother, so it makes sense to me that coming out meant breaking the silence about my family pain."

After a tumultuous struggle to come out as gay, David was quick to realize that his family issues were very significant in how he felt about himself.

David left home as soon as he was able to make it on his own. He graduated from high school at seventeen, but because he still needed to be the *"good boy,"* he waited until he was given permission to leave at eighteen. He had become involved in a fundamentalist religious group, and once he was eighteen he moved into a religious community. He was there six months and then moved across the country to join another religious commune, where he lived for the next four years.

DAVID:

"I ran away as far as possible. I told myself that it was all over. I continued to deny my sexual feelings. I joined religious groups that treated sex with as much fear and loathing as I did. I thought I had safely tucked myself away from facing my sexuality, but the fantasies continued. And this led to even greater feelings of guilt."

David says he spent those four years trying to quell all of his feelings, trying to believe that God had not made him gay. Any feelings he had became sublimated in the belief that he was a disciple of brotherly love.

At twenty-one, David left the religious community. He says he left without a lot of thought or insight — he simply knew that he was terribly unhappy. He next enrolled in a liberal but religious college, which led him gradually to release his extreme "all or nothing" thinking. It was at this college that he heard a professor speak of gays without negative judgment. This was a first. The professor first said that due to his religious beliefs he'd been against homosexuality. But then he'd had to confront the fact that two of his dearest friends were gay and that he loved them. Once the issue became personalized, he said he had to rethink theology. This was the beginning for David.

"It was my first experience with that kind of thinking. It was my first hint that it was okay to be gay."

David then transferred to a secular school. There he recognized many students who were gay. But he still wasn't ready to handle so much exposure, and he transferred to a Catholic college. Not until then did he learn that his dearest high school friend was also gay.

"The first person I had ever loved was to become the first person I would have a physical experience with. That was when I was finally able to face myself.

"I began therapy. I was discovering my true self. I began to experiment with the word gay and eventually to use it proudly to define an aspect of myself that had so profoundly influenced my life. Several years after that, I began to experiment with a new set of words: Adult Child of an Alcoholic. I soon learned that being raised in an alcoholic home was the cause of my frequent depressions and confusion. That, too, was a coming-out process."

Like many homosexual Adult Children, David came to feel proud to define himself as gay. But resolving his Adult Child issues was an ongoing struggle.

Jean did not begin her coming-out process until her early thirties. By then her active addiction to alcohol made it even more difficult.

When Jean graduated from high school, she decided to go to a women's college, hoping to find an atmosphere in which she could feel accepted for who she was.

JEAN:

"I liked the idea of all those women in one place, and I had great hopes of meeting others who were also interested in women. However, I did not meet any other lesbians, although I'm sure there must have been some there who were in the closet. I had crushes on other women, but I pushed those feelings away and dated guys.

"I never felt as if I fit in with the other students, although I tried. A sexually addicted friend suggested that all I needed was to get 'screwed.' So I began to pursue a sexually active, promiscuous life-style for a few months, sleeping with some of the local college men.

"Finally, at twenty-three I experienced the thrill of sex with a woman. I will never forget the elation and the intensity of my feelings. But the liaison was very secret. We didn't even discuss it. We pretended that nothing was going on.

"I kept my sexual orientation very secret and continued to date men. My longest-term relationships were with married men. I even convinced myself that if I got married, my preference for women would go away. My drinking was also progressing strongly at this point.

"Through my twenties, I established and maintained several very close friendships with one or two women at a time. I felt attracted to them, but I vowed that I would never ruin the friendship by expressing my attraction. However, when I was thirty one of my women friends and I became lovers. We had been in a co-dependent relationship for three years, supporting each other's progressive alcohol abuse and exploring what it meant to be lesbian and scared in the Midwest in 1979. Alcoholism ultimately brought an end to our relationship.

"After another three-year relationship ended, I entered therapy. I was tired of repeating the same patterns in relationships, and had I thought that the therapist was a recovering alcoholic who specialized in substance abuse, I think I would have tried to find another therapist. I wasn't about to give up my alcohol, nor was I willing to admit or accept the fact that I was an alcoholic. But she accepted my life-style and could understand my issues with lesbian relationships. That felt more important than the alcohol at the time."

Jean would need to get clean and sober before she could address her Adult Child issues and become self-accepting. Her therapist knew this, but she also understood that if she confronted Jean about her alcoholism before Jean had decided to trust her, Jean would run from therapy. It takes a finely skilled therapist to judge the timing correctly, but she did. The therapist's acceptance of Jean as a person was pivotal to Jean's remaining in therapy and to her ultimate acceptance of and surrender to her chemical dependency.

"Eventually, with my therapist's help, I was able to admit that I was not in control of my chemical use and abuse. I attended a Cocaine Anonymous meeting and then went to my first AA meeting. I was terrified. I was sure all 'real' alcoholics would remind me of my father. But no one reminded me of my father. Everyone hugged me and accepted me, even though I was alcoholic and gay. This was when my real recovery began."

Jean had struggled to come out when she was actively addicted to alcohol. However, as a clean and sober person she can now continue her coming-out process without the other issues getting in the way. When you are addicted, your thinking is distorted, often delusional. You cannot make healthy decisions for yourself. Your choices are limited. People are just as (if not more) apt to respond to you in disgust, confusion, anger, or fear as an addicted person as they are to you as a homosexual.

John's coming-out process began in his teens, and it has been slow and gradual. It was important for him to come out to his parents. In his progression coming-out, John was more influenced by his parents' acceptance than were the other people in this book. After he had told his parents, he was better able to work through his own conflict about bisexuality and homosexuality. All this was made possible by the fact that John's parents had entered recovery during his teenage years and the family had become much more child-centered. Even though the children were older at that point, these circumstances probably greatly influenced John's need for his parents acceptance.

JOHN:

"Growing up as a gay, alcoholic, addict, and Child of an Alcoholic, I felt as if my ticket was pretty full. At the age of twenty-one, when I was starting to get sober, I still had problems dealing with my sexuality. I was extremely homophobic, extremely paranoid. I felt

isolated. I didn't want to hurt anybody. I felt that any expression of sexuality — by being me — would destroy the family and cause pain and shame and anger. I did everything to cover up. I dated women. I had dates for every event."

While John was in residential treatment for his addiction, his father came up for family day. This is when John told his father about his sexuality.

"I was so scared to tell him that I had three counselors in the room. I told my dad about me, how I felt, and what my fears were. My father told me that he had known about my sexuality for about three years. We sat and cried, and then we went for a walk, arm in arm, and it was really nice. After treatment we went home and told my mom. Actually I told her I was bisexual because I do enjoy women and enjoy being sexual with women."

What John has described is a process for both individuals and families in active recovery where new and healthy rules are practiced. These are

• Break the *"Don't talk"* rule. Speak the truth.
• Express your feelings.
• Offer and allow yourself to receive support.
• Take responsibility for yourself.

Over the next couple of years John came to accept that, as much as he enjoyed and was able to be intimate with women, his true sexual orientation was as a gay man.

"Living as a gay man, I know what it is to own an important part of myself that society condemns or ignores. It can be difficult enough dealing with your sexual orientation when you're growing up, but an alcoholic parent adds further complications and hardships. Today I like me. I know I am gay, not bisexual, and I have far less shame or fear telling others of my homosexuality."

Gays and lesbians know very well that the coming-out process is ongoing. Often one has to confront it on a daily basis. With each new person one meets, one must decide if owning one's sexual identity is relevant. Then one must decide whether or not to reveal it. Most gays and lesbians have developed a finely tuned internal radar mechanism that they perpetually scan, asking, *"Is it safe to be me?"* For those who have grown up in a chemically dependent family, the Adult Child issue of being hypervigilant refines this skill even further. Nevertheless, this is an incredible emotional burden, and it requires a lot of energy to maintain.

Unfortunately there is an assumption that most people are heterosexual unless they say otherwise.

JOHN:

"What is different about us is invisible. Because it is invisible, we're often subjected to cruel, hurtful statements from others who don't realize they're being insulting."

Gays and lesbians deserve to go through life with the dignity and respect due all human beings — regardless of sexual orientation.

ADULTHOOD AND RECOVERY

ADRIENNE

Age: 33
Partner Status: Relationship five years, parent of young child
Occupation: Music industry
Recovery Process: Al-Anon, ACOA, therapy

At age thirty-three Adrienne has been in a relationship for five years now. She is also the parent of a two-year-old son. She has been actively working on her recovery process for six years.

Adrienne moved to New York from the Midwest to work in the women's music industry for a performer who was herself a recovering alcoholic.

ADRIENNE:

"She promptly Twelve-Stepped me into ACOA/Al-Anon. Beginning my recovery work was difficult. I was a total co-dependent and workaholic, throwing myself into managing other people's lives and careers for very low wages. It took six years and a combination of my recovery program, good therapy, and intuitive work to have what I enjoy today — an interesting and successful business as a talent agent, a happy and healthy five-year relationship with my lover and our two-year-old son."

She describes the process of recovery as gradual and at times painful.

"Ultimately, though, it has been very gratifying. While I can still put other people's needs first, it wasn't an automatic response anymore. Under stress I occasionally worry about catastrophe ruining my life, but I don't assume it will. I have learned to express anger directly and set clear boundaries and limits around what I will and won't do. I have a sense of humor and perspective about myself and

feel mostly amused, rather than controlled, by irrational thoughts or fears. I no longer gravitate toward active alcoholics, co-dependents, and addicts as friends and associates; instead I choose recovering addicts, alkies, and co-dependents.

"I used to worry that I would be poor all my life, since I believed I was too stupid to be successful in business. Today, by using my ACOA traits—being responsible, organized, self-sufficient, a good problem-solver, guide, and manager of people's lives — I have a successful career."

Adrienne says that the denial of her feelings, which she carried well into her late twenties, is gone now. She is no longer numb and defended. She no longer overeats to cover up loneliness, isolation, and fear.

Recently Adrienne has been doing another significant layer of recovery work.

"Lately I've begun to remember being violently sexually abused by my stepfather. This memory surprised me, but it makes sense, given some of the difficulties I have with being sexually present, a lingering feeling of unexplainable shame, and a basic distrust and fear.

"During the abuse he would tell me he would kill me if I told anyone. Although I know statistically that lesbian and straight women have experienced the same incidence of sexual abuse, I've had to confront on a gut level the stereotype that sexual abuse made me a lesbian. I used to think that there had to be more to my low self-esteem than simply being raised in an alcoholic family. Remembering the abuse provided the answer."

While lesbian women do not appear to have a higher incidence of sexual abuse in their history, people who are sexually abused typically do have significant distrust of males (assuming the perpetrator was male). Yet there is no substantial increase of lesbians among survivors of sexual abuse. Adrienne is a lesbian who experienced childhood sexual abuse.

The ways in which her incest affects her sexually is in her sexual behavior, not in her sexual identity. The shame an incest survivor experiences most often does affect sexual behavior — such as the ability to be sexually present (to not disassociate from the body), to ask for what the partner needs, and to set limits. Adrienne is correct in believing that there was more than alcoholism in the family to create low self-esteem; the incest was not only a major violation of her body, but of her spirit as well.

"I feel honored to be part of a community of people who have overcome emotional and sometimes physical traumas to lead enriched lives. I am grateful to have established a spiritual belief and practice that nourishes and sustains rather than oppresses me.

"Today I'm enjoying the precious experience of parenting. It has been quite a challenge, stimulating issues that I thought were resolved. There is nothing like having a bright, inquisitive, secure, demanding toddler around to push all one's buttons. I have gained a acute understanding of how difficult it is to be a healthy parent when you are not using substances, let alone if you are. I consider myself pretty aware — yet sometimes my partner and I throw up our hands in exasperation or frustration. (The good part is we throw our hands in the air, not at him.)

"I've learned firsthand how vulnerable and dependent little kids are. And this has given me more compassion for how I must have felt. I've also enjoyed vicariously reliving part of my childhood by playing with him and loving and helping him in a way that I missed.

"I am happy and grateful to be a lesbian and to live my life as openly as I do. Today I feel blessed, no longer cursed. There is truly an element of magic in relating intimately to women — a core understanding and connection that arises from simply being female and together."

DAVID

Age: 32
Partner Status: Relationship four years
Occupation: Psychologist
Recovery Process: Therapy

Today, at thirty-two, David has been in a relationship for four years. He has also been in therapy and has been actively working on his ACOA issues.

Initially in the relationship, David found it difficult to deal with his fears of being abandoned, and he was frequently depressed. It took two to three years in therapy, and the patience and stability of his partner, for David to learn to trust.

DAVID:

"I understood healthy relationships in my head, but my fear of being abandoned was so great that my emotions overrode my intellectual understanding. I know these fears were from my childhood. It just took time to overcome them."

After David received his doctorate in clinical psychology, he and his partner moved to a small city, which they are currently enjoying. Moving to a new place often intensifies the issues of coming out.

"As a gay person, I am open and out about my sexuality. I have not come out at my job, but I don't intend to make it a secret. We have already established relationships with other gay couples. I am a member of gay and lesbian organizations. I am on gay and lesbian mailing lists. I am comfortable with being gay, and I know I can live my life personally and professionally as a gay person. Yet I do not immediately tell people my sexual identity. I find that is not always helpful. I've learned to discern the appropriate timing to tell people without having to deny me in the meantime."

David is describing a recovery process of learning to listen to his own cues, to trust and value his perception. To do this, he has had to develop a sense of who he is and what he wants beyond simply reacting to the events of his life. In doing so he is establishing healthy boundaries for himself.

For the most part, David's pain about his family is gone. Today he has a relationship with both of his parents and all of his siblings. He describes himself as the thread that keeps the family together, the link between his parents and the other siblings. He says it is strange to go from feeling like the black sheep to being the favored child. He believes his parents are so relieved that he has left the *"Jesus freak"* world, and so proud of his being the first in his family to earn a Ph.D., that they are grateful for what he's doing for the family.

David laughingly says that his mom may be accepting his homosexuality because he hasn't *"been stolen by another woman."* He believes she always tried to counter the blatant rejection he received from his father as a child. However, possibly as a result of aging, David's father is reaching out more and indicating that he wants to have a relationship with David.

"I can now accept and love my father for who he is. Not that the memories will be forgotten, but I can own those feelings and accept them."

The AIDS issue has affected David's life significantly.

"AIDS is just one more thing that makes me think that life is so difficult. At times I have become very pessimistic and have reverted to my old coping mechanisms by ignoring the issue. I've tried not to talk about my friends who have died from AIDS. I don't hide the fact that I am gay, nor the fact that I am an ACOA. But I do find myself wanting to hide the pain I feel at the tremendous losses I've experienced as a result of the AIDS epidemic. I have to make an active effort to fight the denial.

"In my recovery in general, I am learning to be more assertive and not to overreact to things as much. I can now acknowledge the validity

of my feelings. I'm able to own my rage, love, lust, fear, sadness, and the myriad other human emotions that were blocked out for so many years.

"And yet when I have to deal with personal tragedies in my life, it's still easy to slip back into my old patterns of avoidance and pain. But my intellect and my new coping skills help me do what I need. I struggle against the old familiar response as I forge what I know is a much healthier one. I'm still struggling against 'all or nothing' thinking, and I need people to point that out to me. But I'm getting better. I'm less critical of myself, more aware of my own needs, and much more realistic about my expectations in my relationship.

"Today I have less and less need to define myself through awards and accomplishments. While they're nice, they don't make me a better person. Who I am as a person is what empowers me. And underneath everything, I now know I'm okay just the way I am.

"I'm not a victim any longer. I've learned to recognize my strength. I can affect situations and change how I react to them. I have choices. I feel empowered. All this is very different from my childhood.

"Today I feel a benevolent presence all around me. I really believe I am loved, that I am acceptable. I have gone through most of my life feeling unlovable. Today I trust I am worthy of love. Oh, I can be critical of myself, but I no longer feel worthless."

JEAN

Age: 42
Partner Status: Single
Occupation: Public relations
Recovery Process: AA, therapy

At forty-two Jean is enjoying a successful career as an advertising manager for a major corporation. She has a beautiful home and healthy, supportive friends. Although her parents consider her the *"good child,"* she still struggles with her sense of not being good enough. But with the support of Alcoholics Anonymous and therapy, she is learning to accept herself as she is and to love herself.

JEAN:

"I've been sober for four years now. I've accepted my addictions, and I'm learning how to accept myself. I'm even learning to accept my feelings — at least some of the time. I like myself now. I'm no longer afraid that people will reject me because I am a lesbian. I'm no longer afraid that people will reject me because I'm an alcoholic. My recovery has offered me the opportunity to develop healthy friendships with both heterosexuals and homosexuals. But, even better, now I get most of my acceptance from within.

"Accepting myself hasn't come easily, It's been painful, and I've been rebellious. I've denied and denied and denied — my addictions, my father's alcoholism, my mother's co-dependency, my fear, and my anger.

"However, when I began to participate in an Adult Child therapy group, I learned that it was safe to gradually remove the wall that had kept me separate from myself and from others. I've discovered that the real pain is never as bad as the fear and anticipation of the pain.

"My parents and I remain both physically and emotionally distant. I have a role that I play with them. I am the successful daughter, I'm the good daughter. Not much has changed since I was a kid. I was always afraid that my mother wouldn't love me if she knew who I really was, and I always felt rejected by my alcoholic father. I have never directly told them what was really going on with me, and we still don't discuss my life-style. But what has changed, and what is most important, is that now I'm okay with this."

Jean is not presently in a relationship, but since she's been sober she's had two short relationships.

"At this moment I'm learning to be more honest with myself and my partners. At least now if I get into an unhealthy relationship, I have the sense to get out if it doesn't seem to be workable."

Jean recognizes that the most important thing she can do for herself is to come to terms with the pain she feels.

"To continue to grow, I know I will have to allow myself to be vulnerable. I cannot hold my pain inside any longer. If I don't allow myself to feel the pain, I will simply keep running from it and not dealing with it. So now I'm learning to walk through the pain a step at a time. The things that have been vital to my recovery are my Twelve Step groups, my therapy, and healthy network of friends, and my Higher Power. I have learned to listen to my Higher Power."

KIM

Age: 33
Partner Status: Relationship five years
Occupation: Administrator of nonprofit agency
Recovery Process: ACOA, Al-Anon, CODA, therapy

Kim has actively pursued her recovery in therapy and a Twelve Step program for over seven years. At thirty-three she now lives in northern California, where she is successful in her career as an administrator of a nonprofit helping agency. She is happy in her relationship of five years.

Kim had begun therapy for her depression and was being treated with antidepressants when she met the woman who was to become her next partner.

KIM:

"After the breakup of my first lesbian relationship, which had lasted five years, I soon met someone new. This woman was a recovering alcoholic who quickly directed me to Al-Anon, saying it

would be helpful for us both since I was now the partner of a recovering alcoholic. It was there that I clearly began to identify my Adult Child issues, and this led me to Adult Child self-help and co-dependency groups and to therapy. All of them have been vital in helping me find the answers to my life.

"I think, in some ways, that being lesbian has facilitated my recovery. I went to visit my parents recently — we live two hundred miles apart — and saw lots of relatives I hadn't seen in years. I was struck by something I saw more clearly than ever before — every single woman on my mother's side of the family, a four-generation span, has struggled with some kind of serious mood disorder, mostly severe depression. Upon my return home, I shared this insight with friends, and one of them asked me how I'd escaped. At first I said I hadn't, and I told her about my own severe depression and three years on antidepressants. But then I realized that I really had escaped. And I think being a lesbian had a great deal to do with it. Being surrounded by women helped me value and empower all that I am. Listening to feminist music and exploring a very different culture aided me in rejecting dysfunctional family values and helped me develop new healthy values for myself — after I'd bottomed out.

"Life as a lesbian is for me clearly different from life as a heterosexual. I know that sounds very obvious. But it was a life-saving discovery for me. The times I have felt the craziest, the most suicidal, the most depressed, was when I could not see how I was different from my mother and sister. The only choices I thought I had then seemed to be either suicide or alcoholism. Affirming my lesbianism gave me more choices, more options, more of a chance for a positive outcome."

Kim says she believes she still carries some emotional burdens of the family that she might not if she weren't lesbian.

"My sister's suicide leaves me the only girl child in the family. Chances are I will never have a child, or if I do, it will create a complex family issue. I have some feelings of regret about that. Some grieving

*comes up periodically that is tied in with the ACOA 'responsible child'
struggle that I'm still fighting.*

"Along the same lines, I think about other things with sadness, like
not having a more accepted kind of wedding or household. There's
also something in there about wanting to show my parents that I'm
normal, that I'm happy. That I did okay. I know they blame themselves
for my sister's death — as I did for a long time — and I want to show
them they did the best they could as parents. How they handle my
lesbianism is an integral part of how they feel as parents, and for them
that is negative. Part of the Adult Child issues I'm still working on is
trying to protect my parents from me and themselves.

"So, where am I now? I'm very happy. I spent several years in
therapy and have been in and around Twelve Step recovery programs
for four years. My primary external compulsion has been
workaholism, something that continues to surface every now and then.
The only chemical I ever abused was nicotine. which I recently quit.
I've been in a relationship almost five years now with the woman I
intend to spend my life with. I have a good solid career.

"My parents and I are on good terms. My mother's chemical
dependency is still a family secret. But I don't push it into the open
like I used to, and she doesn't drink around me. My parents accept my
life-style and even sent a birthday card to my lover this year. Happy
endings are possible — for those who want them."

> # JOHN:
>
> Age: 28
> Partner Status: Single
> Occupation: Chemical dependency specialist
> Additional: Parents in recovery today
> Recovery Process: AA, therapy

Six years clean and sober, at twenty-eight John is a chemical dependency counselor in Colorado.

Five years ago John suffered a series of illnesses and lost a great deal of weight. He had chronic fatigue, swollen glands, and was experiencing wide mood swings. Finally he was diagnosed with ARC (AIDS-related complex).

JOHN:

"I felt as if I were dying. I had no control. So I placated and adjusted and took care of everyone else. I hid how I felt and what I thought. I hid my fears because I didn't want anyone to worry about me. I tried to take care of other people so that they would be okay with my illness.

"I feared for my family. I was afraid that because I was gay, because I was an alcoholic, because I was an addict, and now because I had ARC, they would be hurt. I was afraid of what this might do to them, how they would be affected by this.

"When I found out, I called Mom and Dad and told them that I was very sick. They flew up to be with me and were very supportive. We all learned as much as we could about the disease. But I felt so much despair at the time that I was planning to kill myself. I had even made all the preparations for ending my life, but my mother kept calling me every day, asking me if I had seen a doctor.

"Finally I went to a doctor, who hooked me up with a therapist. With the therapist's help I worked through my suicidal feelings and set out to discover my own identity. I began to reevaluate, reframe, and relearn. I discovered how to get in touch with my inner child and the experiences of my childhood, and this helped clarify my needs today as an adult.

"The characteristics of being an Adult Child with ARC and Adult Child who is gay are the same. The emotions are the same. ARC is simply another set of circumstances in which I must be responsible for myself. For a while I was blaming God because He was putting me through yet another dark time. I almost totally lost any sense of Higher Power that I'd gotten from my Twelve Step program. I kept thinking, Why did God do this to me?

"As part of my ACOA recovery, I have to take responsibility for my health. There is no changing it. There is no denying it. It is real."

John has been able to look at his ARC as an opportunity to examine his life more deeply. But before he could do that, he responded very normally with denial, anger, blame and depression. Ultimately he has come to acceptance. This is a process he may repeat several times. But John had some tools as a result of his participation in recovery from both his alcoholism and his ACOA issues that would help him to confront his illness and go on living his life, instead of seeing himself as dying.

Regardless of what is happening physically, there are still choices you can make about your life.

"Today I know that God is not punishing me by giving me this illness. It is not my fault. And the illness is not my identity. I am not a bad person because I have ARC. God and I are in this together, and He is still a power greater than anything I know. Most of the time I am grateful for what I am able to learn.

"Unfortunately there still has to be the secrecy. There are times when I cannot be open with people about what is going on with me.

"I used to share my pain with people in order to take theirs away. But I don't do that today. Their pain is theirs, and my pain is mine. Their pain is no greater than mine because they are experiencing it. I don't have to take it away. And I don't have to share my illness for pity. In fact, I don't share it with most people because I don't want it to be the focus of 'How are you?' "

As many Adult Children are doing today, John is learning to have healthy relationships.

"While I'm not in a primary relationship, I feel capable of being in a healthy relationship. In the past I experienced sex without much honesty or intimacy. Today I'm working on getting to know the other person and allowing the other person to get to know me. That doesn't happen in five minutes. I want the other person to be able to say he likes me, that he likes how I treat myself and him, that he is comfortable with my health issues. Honesty is vital and practicing safe sex is automatic in my recovery."

Adult children have spent years keeping perceptions and feelings a secret, guessing at what other people want, attempting to get approval, and communicating in a distorted manner. The result often produces both chaos and excitement. But maintaining this fever-pitch emotional environment also means maintaining dysfunctional ways of being.

"I still struggle with my need for chaos and excitement. But I am no longer isolated. I am no longer invisible to myself and others. I can look at myself in the mirror, I take care of myself. I've been working out, I eat properly, and I sleep well. I feel good about myself, my work and my life.

"I've also been working on my own homophobia. I'm talking more openly about who I am. I'm tired of changing my pronouns and lowering my voice to sound more masculine to fit what people want. I want to be acknowledged, not discounted. I want the same respect that anyone else gets. If I'm in a restaurant with another man, I want

to be acknowledged the same way a heterosexual couple would be. I want polite respect.

Today if someone asks me if I'm married, I say, 'No, I am gay.' I like that."

What John is describing is the Adult Child recovery process of learning to value oneself and to live one's life without chronic fear. Recovery is about healthy risk taking, and John is clearly taking those risks. Although he may be fearful initially, he is being more honest with himself and others, and this enhances his self-esteem.

"Now that I'm no longer in denial, I know that I have felt a great deal of pain in my life. But one of the reasons I know this is because I also feel so much love and pleasure. With this new understanding of myself, I feel so much room for growth, so much desire to be at peace with myself. I don't want to wait for death to bring me peace. I'm striving to find that peace today and every day of my life."

RECOVERY CONSIDERATIONS

Adrienne, John, Kim, David, and Jean were all raised in actively chemically dependent families. All but one recognized their sexual orientation in their preadolescent or adolescent years, adding to their sense of:

- Never being good enough.
- Feeling different.
- Feeling shame and quilt.

Today all five proudly embrace their sexual identities. They recognize the impact of chemical dependency on their lives and have begun a process that not only facilitates the healing of childhood wounds, but offers them the respect they deserve as human beings regardless of their sexual orientation.

Because of the *"double duty"* — the synergistic effect of being gay or lesbian and an Adult Child — it may take a bit longer to feel safe enough to begin and maintain one's recovery work. It is important that gay and lesbian Adult Children be very caring and patient with themselves. While you have the same issues as heterosexual Adult Children, you may find the following considerations especially relevant to your recovery process.

Self-Acceptance

All Adult Children must work on developing greater self-acceptance. This awakens as we begin to develop compassion and empathy for ourselves as children. Once we own the child within, the vulnerable, innocent child fully deserving of validation, it will be hard to see any of the ugliness or depravity that gays and lesbians often learn to associate with themselves. That sense of wrongness and shame has come from messages internalized from those who are themselves frightened and confused about sexuality. Just because they were taught that homosexuality is bad doesn't mean that it is bad. Sexual orientation is not bad; it just is.

Self-acceptance and self-love also mean addressing one's own homophobia. The messages gays and lesbians constantly hear are that homosexuals are sick, dirty, immoral, ugly. Having to contend with the pressures of external homophobia on a day-to-day basis is at best disheartening. But dealing with internalized homophobia is even more difficult and painful. Gays and lesbians often learn to accept homophobic values. They believe that because they are different, there is something wrong with them. This is demonstrated by David, who sought a counselor so he could become heterosexual; by Jean, who believed that her feelings were wrong; and by David, who prayed that he would change.

One significant aspect of recovery means addressing this internal homophobia, because it is impossible to experience recovery while rejecting oneself. Homosexual or not, if people are homophobic, their choices of responding to others and to life are limited and compromised.

Isolation

Because gay and lesbian Adult Children have lived so much of their lives "not talking" about the real issues, they are even more isolated, both emotionally and socially, than most ACOAs. They have less trust in the process of being open and honest about their feelings and perceptions. Even when they're highly motivated to be more honest with themselves and others, the layers of protection can only be lifted slowly.

It is common to find many gays and lesbians who do not appear to be socially isolated. However, their friendships will often be segmented. They will share certain parts of their lives, but not others, such as whom they live with, whom they love. Although this serves to protect, it can be very isolating emotionally. To avoid such a segmented life, many homosexuals become even more socially isolated, relating only to a very small number of people they can be open with. Isolation often becomes habitual, and many gays and lesbians learn to discount their loneliness by deluding themselves into thinking that isolation is *"alone time."* A certain amount of alone time is healthy, but it can easily become an unhappy escape.

Because of greater feelings of differentness, it is important to have the opportunity for validation of perceptions and experiences that often can only be offered by other gays and lesbians who are in recovery. It helps to lessen homophobia, both internal and external, and it offers one the opportunity to see homosexuals as bright, capable, insightful, and sensitive — and just as good at practicing self-care and having healthy relationships as heterosexuals.

Most homosexuals find that they benefit from both gay/lesbian and heterosexual support groups. These groups may be based in either traditional therapy or self-help. Gay and lesbian community organizations may be able to direct one to *"recovering communities"* and other social resources. It is important for anyone in recovery to understand that in life in general we cannot get all of our needs met by one person or in one place. The path to self-acceptance and recovery will involve a number of resources.

Reaching out, becoming less isolated, eases homophobia — it lessens fear, loneliness, and shame. It is the beginning of recovery.

Reflection And Abandonment

As young children, ACOAs live with chronic fear of abandonment. As homosexuals in a heterosexual society, gays and lesbians are constantly being rejected for any and all aspects of who they are simply because of their sexual orientation. Being homosexual means living with a heightened likelihood of rejection and/or abandonment. Yet there are gays and lesbians willing to offer support, and there are growing numbers of heterosexuals who accept gay or lesbian individuals for who they are.

The Adult Child issue of *"not trusting"* can interfere with one's willingness to come out, when in fact the acceptance may be readily available. By addressing this issue directly, gay or lesbian Adult Children have a more realistic opportunity to assess the fears that relate to their homosexuality.

Adult Children are known for their hypervigilance. If they have experienced a lot of rejection in their lives, they will be hypervigilant about any future possibilities of rejection. Most gays and lesbians have had to learn how to defend themselves emotionally against possible rejection. But there's an added dynamic here. The double duty of being both homosexual and an Adult Child may prompt one to read rejection into an encounter when, in fact, it is not occurring. The Adult Child needs to check out any concerns he or she may have. Because of this hypersensitivity, Adult Children tend to set others up, to test their loyalty. Therefore they need to examine these feelings and discuss their fears. The truth is that sometimes rejection is occurring and other times it is not.

Need For Approval

A common characteristic of Adult Children is seeking approval. Being raised in a dysfunctional family denies them the validation and approval they need to develop an internal validation system or positive self-esteem. This is why they continue to seek approval from others as adults. Three cautions might be helpful here.

• First, it is possible that as a gay or lesbian, the need for approval is so great that one can be indiscriminate in disclosing their homosexuality and as a result set themself up for being rejected or abandoned.

• Second, it is possible that this need for approval may prompt the gay or lesbian to pass as a heterosexual and develop only segmented relationships.

• Third, it is possible that out of fear of rejection, the gay or lesbian will build a defensive wall and reject opportunities in which others could offer approval and acceptance.

Recovery means learning how to become *"self-approving."* It means inviting healthy people into your life who will offer approving messages. What is hurtful is being dependent on others to make you feel good about yourself. As you seek friendships within both the healthy gay and lesbian community and the healthy heterosexual community, you will find others who will be approving.

Nevertheless, it is vital to keep working on your ability to affirm and empower yourself. Don't rely on any one person for all of your outside validation. It isn't fair to that person, nor is it fair to you. There are many others who can and will offer validation, and you will blossom even more as your network of healthy support grows.

Differentness

Heterosexual Adult Children in recovery often say they no longer have the sense of differentness or separateness from others that had so characterized their growing-up years. They claim that the *"alone in the crowd"* syndrome disappears.

As gays and lesbians move on in their recovery process, the sense of being separate and different also lessens. Yet their sexual orientation does make them members of a minority population. In that respect they will differ from other ACOAs.

However, one vital distinction is very important in recovery. In the past, being different was equated with shame. In recovery one discovers that being different does not mean one is bad. At this point one needs to become comfortable with one's differentness. In addition, the tendency for Adult Children to view the world with an *"all or nothing"* perspective can make them feel even more negative about being different. But once this view of the world begins to open up, it becomes easier and easier to see how similar they are to other people in spite of the differences. Homosexual or heterosexual, we all have the same needs and deserve the same as everyone else.

Coming Out

Coming Out In General

Honesty is integral to Adult Child recovery. Recovery cannot work with selective honesty. Yet that doesn't mean we have to share everything with everyone. Being honest means first learning to be honest with yourself. Then it means choosing environments that feel safe so that you can be true to yourself. Part of the recovery process is learning to discriminate whom we share information with and what is appropriate to share.

You deserve to live life free of fear and free of shame. One way to do that is to begin the coming-out process. On the one hand, honesty is not necessarily easy. On the other, one pays a very high price — one's integrity — by continuing to be dishonest. Many gays and lesbians have come to believe that being honest with oneself and the world is much easier than remaining in the closet.

Living a closeted life means attending weddings, funerals, and family occasions alone or inviting a member of the opposite sex to be with you to keep up the pretense. It means lying about who you are when applying for jobs or credit or buying a house. Blatantly lying throughout one's daily life takes an incredible toll on one's self-esteem.

When one grows up with unpredictability, the ability to compartmentalize is often well developed. Although compartmentalizing one's life from a fear of homophobia is sometimes necessary, it may also be an Adult Child habit that may not be as necessary as we think.

Coming out often means being honest about the one aspect of who you are that you've felt the greatest shame about and have fought the hardest to keep secret. It is difficult to trust the value or the safety of the process of coming out in a homophobic society. And as an Adult Child, you may have even greater difficulty trusting or finding value in honesty.

However, some gay and lesbian Adult Children find that recovery begins by first addressing their sexuality. Typically, once the *"rule of silence"* has been broken in one area, it loosens up other areas and allows one to discover new insights. Heterosexual Adult Children don't usually begin their recovery by revealing their deepest secret. So if you begin your recovery process by coming out, you need to acknowledge the courage that this process takes. Other Adult Children get to start with smaller truths, and some gays and lesbians begin their recovery in a time frame that allows them to come out gradually.

Although being gay or lesbian adds to the pain and struggle of being an Adult Child, there are many ways in which dealing with one issue can have a positive effect on dealing with the other.

David said that when he went into therapy for help with being gay or to change his being gay — he wasn't sure which — it was the second time he'd heard that it was *"fine"* to be gay. All he needed was to hear it again, and he was willing to accept it. He said at that point he gave up his struggle and began to come out. But he adds that the process of accepting who he was opened up Pandora's box. He had to face how he'd come to be so fearful of his feelings, how he'd come to hate himself, and how he'd come to feel so different.

David said he'd thought those issues were the result of being gay, and yet he knew his heterosexual brother had the same issues. Coming out as gay forced David to deal with being an Adult Child.

Jean said that once she had accepted herself as a lesbian, her ACOA issues of isolation and feeling different could be dealt with. She is also aware that recovery from her co-dependency issues will allow her to have healthy relationships.

This is not meant to imply that working on ACOA issues will automatically make being gay or lesbian more comfortable. Jean points out that while she can work on her fear of rejection and abandonment as an ACOA, she still has to confront the reality that being lesbian means she continues to risk a higher level of rejection and abandonment from others.

Many gays and lesbians reflect that the coming-out process is usually much more distressful at the beginning than it is over time. Remember, you're the one who decides whom it is safe to share this information with. You don't have to begin with the person whose approval is most important to you. You don't have to pick the person who frightens you the most.

When heterosexual Adult Children begin their recovery process, they're usually doing it with strangers. They seek a counselor, a therapist, or a self-help group. Often they don't find support or validation from the members of their family or origin or even present-day family members. In addition, they have friends who care about them, but who don't really understand what they're going through. You may want to begin your coming-out process with a gay or lesbian counselor or therapist who is sensitive to these issues or with a gay or lesbian social group or a self-help group.

While the decision to come out is often fraught with stress, many people experience relief and exhilaration as they come out. It relieves the hurtful energy that has burdened them for so long. When one can get beyond the society fears and stigmas, being gay or lesbian becomes as normal to the homosexual as being heterosexual is to those who are straight. It is the homophobia, internal and external, that is so painful.

Choosing the right environment is important. Some areas of the country and some communities are generally more supportive, and others are more homophobic — especially rural areas or smaller cities. Gays and lesbians owe it to themselves to find places where it is safe to own who they are and where they can receive validation and support. Telephone hot lines and gay and lesbian resource centers in major cities can often offer suggestions.

Coming Out To The Family

In coming out to family members, Adult Children need to keep in mind that their family most likely has little or no history of positive affirmation of sexual behavior in general, let alone homosexuality. In dysfunctional families heterosexual sex, which is the perceived society norm, is rarely talked about or portrayed positively. Consequently, when the subject of homosexuality arises, there is even less likelihood of a positive response.

If your family wasn't very accepting of you when they thought you were heterosexual, it will be all the more difficult for you to believe that they will be able to accept you as a gay or lesbian. But remember, the issue here isn't so much your sexual orientation as it their inability to be accepting in general. Chemically dependent families are characteristically critical of and quick to blame others. These are families characterized by denial, not speaking the truth, minimizing, rationalizing. Family members are not used to speaking of sadness and fears about little everyday things and finding support.

Often the time one comes out to family members is the first time that any honesty has taken place in the group. One is telling a major secret with little or no practice to people with no history of favorable reactions to even little secrets. While there's no one right way to come out to one's family, this is the first time there has been any direct and honest communication — remember that a negative response could result as much from the shock of honesty to the dysfunctional family system as from homophobia.

Some gays and lesbians decide not to formally come out to their parents or siblings, and this may be a healthy decision. For others, those who are socially isolated from parents and siblings by choice, the prospect of coming out with one's sexuality is an easy and healthy decision. Yet another choice is to be involved in the lives of parents and siblings and include one's partner in those relationships without ever stating the facts. Many gays and lesbians say they find acceptance from family members if the facts remain unspoken. Coming out and saying, *"I am lesbian/gay"* or, *"I sleep with him (or her),"* could set up the family to react in a way that would not allow the relationship to be as comfortable as it is.

As you experience Adult Child recovery, you become more aware of your needs, and you can identify your feelings. This means that you can establish healthier boundaries and find greater self-acceptance. When you no longer view life from an all-or-nothing perspective, you become more trusting of your perceptions, and you can ascertain a greater range of options. With recovery, the coming-out process is made easier, and the right path for you can evolve in a healthy way.

Acquired Immune Deficiency Syndrome — AIDS

While thousands have died from AIDS, many people are struggling through various stages of acceptance with their illness. Having a chronic and potentially fatal illness is a major issue in and of itself. Knowing that you will not be able to live your life to full term, that your life is being taken away before you have achieved what you have desired, is a stunning loss.

Much work has taken place around the issue of learning to accept such a prognosis. We know that the first reaction is denial. After that comes four more stages: anger, bargaining, depression, and, finally, acceptance. If one is infected with HIV and is an unrecovered Adult Child, this process is all the more difficult. Adult Children may use the denial skills they developed in their dysfunctional families to get stuck in the denial stage and never find peace or acceptance. They may also become very self-destructive as a result of being overwhelmed with their feelings for the first time.

Other ACOA issues can seriously interfere with proper treatment. Having learned not to ask questions could severely limit medical options. The inability to ask for help could make the process more difficult physically and very lonely emotionally. Not having come to terms with parents or siblings could create a powerful emotional and/or financial burden. Not trusting one's perceptions could interfere with using important medical information to one's best advantage, and most important of all, it could deeply affect the choice of how to continue to live one's life.

Often the first time people take a long, hard look at their lives is when their health is seriously threatened. In recovery from ACOA issues or alcoholism, many people have been able to find gifts at a time when others perceive only painful loss. Regardless of what is happening physically, there are still choices you can make about your life. If you haven't begun a recovery process as an ACOA, or if you are chemically dependent, it's never too late to begin. Do not wait. Many benefits come with recovery that will allow you to make sense out of your illness and help you to take charge of your life at least.

To lose a friend, a significant other, or a life partner is tragic. To lose many friends in a relatively short time span can be overwhelming. Under such stress, many adult children resort to old defense mechanisms — they shut down, numb out, and isolate themselves. To handle the grief, some of that is necessary. Even denial has its uses. But, ultimately, in order to cope in a healthy manner, you need to walk through the process of grief. To do that you must know and trust your feelings; and you must include others in your process. Without some Adult Child recovery it will be difficult to grieve the loss of friends and/or partners. Some people discover that this crisis may be the starting point of recovery from Adult Child issues.

Do not isolate yourself during this time. Reach out. Talk about your anger. But be aware that the anger is not about being homosexual — it is about the disease, about the AIDS virus taking loved ones away. Talk about your hurt, the gut-wrenching pain. Talk about your fears. Talk about the joys you have had with your friends and loved ones. Precious gifts can come out of the process of sharing honestly with a friend who is so ill — gifts for both of you.

Relationships

In many ways homosexual Adult Children aren't any different from heterosexual Adult Children when it comes to relationships. Most people who have been raised in troubled families have difficulty in relationships. They often engage in personal relationships that do not meet their needs, where communication is hurtful and distorted and everyone has different goals. At times they are in abusive, violent relationships.

Remember, Adult Children come from families where it has not been safe to talk openly and honestly. They haven't learned to trust; they often have not learned to negotiate or problem-solve. Many times they have not learned how to share. Some ACOAs have learned intrusiveness and disrespect of others' boundaries. Others have learned to tolerate inappropriate behavior and often find themselves victimized. This certainly does not lay the groundwork for a healthy relationship.

In relationships between unrecovered Adult Children, both partners often come from a shame-based background without the skills to create a healthy environment. There is also the added dynamic of living in a homophobic society that reinforces the conflict homosexual couples experience in trying to stay together and work out issues. It's hard enough for heterosexual couples to do this, but there are even fewer positive reinforcements or expectations for homosexual couples.

Nevertheless, tumultuous relationships among gays and lesbians do not have to be the norm. With recovery from Adult Child issues, you can invite healthier people into your life and come to have healthy expectations for relationships. There are gay and lesbian couples who have lived together for many years in highly successful relationships. Although they tend to be less visible to the younger population, they are there, and seeking them out as positive role models is always helpful.

Healthy Adult Children choose partners with whom they can enter into mutual agreements. They are respectful of their own boundaries — of what feels safe and good — and are equally respectful of others and their boundaries. This is true whatever the sexual ordination may be.

A significant and hurtful dynamic in a gay or lesbian relationship is the potential for invalidation when it's not safe to come out as a couple. The inability to feel safe in having your partner join you at a social event at work, with your family, or in the community can create a strain on the relationship. Even when partners attend social events together as a couple, it may not feel safe to openly touch in tenderness or support. You may have to lie when you introduce your partner. Going to social events as a couple is often a setup for rejection. And every time this occurs, you have to deal with the implicit message that a homosexual relationship is wrong. These circumstances often force gays and lesbians in relationships to participate in social events separately or not at all. Yet one of the joys of a relationship is sharing — both the good times and the hard times. A circumscribed life is frustrating. Homosexual ACOAs continually have to make compromises that heterosexual ACOAs do not have to make.

Because of this, homosexuals in a relationship need to work even harder at being available to one another as a support. Communication is even more necessary. Knowing what your feelings are and finding appropriate expression for them is vital. Problem-solving skills are another important requisite. Adult Child recovery offers gays and lesbians new skills that give them a greater range of choices in their lives.

You don't have to live a life plagued with always having to be socially separate from your partner. Today you can choose to spend time with those who will offer you and your partner support and validation and meet your interpersonal needs. There are other gays and lesbians and heterosexuals who will lovingly accept you for who you are. But before you allow such people in your life, you will usually have to confront your own internal homophobia first. Remember, the people we choose to be around reflect the person inside us.

Chemical Dependence

We know now that Children of Alcoholics are more likely to become chemically dependent. Research indicates that daughters of chemically dependent families are two times more likely to become chemically dependent; sons are five times more likely to become chemically dependent. Research also suggests that a gay or lesbian person is two to three times more likely to become chemically dependent. Therefore being both and Adult Child and homosexual warrants special caution in regard to alcohol and other drug usage. Anyone wanting to assess his alcohol or drug usage should use the *"Do You Have the Disease of Alcoholism?"* self-assessment test in the appendix. This is an objective tool that can help you keep yourself honest and healthy.

Remember, chemical dependency is a primary illness. Until it is addressed, it will be difficult to work on Adult Child issues and even more difficult to work on gay or lesbian issues. But also remember that, chemical dependency is treatable. Thousands of gays and lesbians are clean and sober today. They have dealt with all the fears about what it means to have a sober life. There are gay and lesbian self-help meetings of Alcoholics Anonymous, and there are gay and lesbian-oriented treatment programs. It is also a fact that many gays and lesbians experience a wonderful recovery while attending mainstream Twelve Step groups.

Putting Fear And Shame Behind You

Nobody deserves to live with shame and fear because of growing up in an alcoholic family. Certainly no one deserves to live with shame because of a specific sexual orientation. Adult Child recovery means putting the fears and shame of your childhood behind you. It means challenging hurtful belief systems and learning healthier skills. It means valuing yourself, believing in yourself. Each of us is very special. Each of us deserves to believe that in our hearts. I believe that when gay and lesbian Adult Children address their issues, they experience greater opportunities to be true to themselves.

"Today I believe I am acceptable.
Today I trust I am worthy of Love."

Lesbian Adult Child

APPENDIX

THE ORIGINAL LAUNDRY LIST FOR ADULT CHILDREN OF ALCOHOLICS

The Problem

The Characteristics we seem to have in common due to our being brought up in an alcoholic household:

A. We became isolated and afraid of people and authority figures.

B. We became approval seekers and lost our identity in the process.

C. We are frightened by angry people and any personal criticism.

D. We either become alcoholics, marry them, or both, or find another compulsive personality such as a workaholic to fulfill our sick abandonment needs.

E. We live life from the viewpoint of victims and are attracted by that weakness in our lives and friendship relationships.

F. We have an overdeveloped sense of responsibility and it is easier for us to be concerned with others rather than ourselves; this enables us not too look too closely at our own faults, etc.

G. We get guilt feelings when we stand up for ourselves instead of giving in to others.

H. We become addicted to excitement.

I. We confuse love and pity and tend to "love" people we can "pity" and "rescue."

J. We have stuffed our feelings from our traumatic childhoods and have lost the ability to feel or express our feelings because it hurts so much. (Denial)

K. We judge ourselves harshly and have a very low sense of self-esteem.

L. We are dependent personalities who are terrified of abandonment and will do anything to hold on to a relationship in order not to experience painful abandonment feelings which we received from living with sick people who were never there emotionally for us.

M. Alcoholism is a family disease and we became para-alcoholics and took on the characteristics of that disease even though we did not pick up the drink.

N. Para-alcoholics are reactors rather than actors.

The Solution

By attending Adult Children of Alcoholics meetings on a regular basis, we learn that we can live our lives in a more meaningful manner; we learn to change our attitudes and old patterns of behavior and habits, to find serenity, even happiness.

A. Alcoholism is a three-fold disease; mental, physical, and spiritual. Our parents are victims of this disease which either ends in death or insanity. This is the beginning of the gift of forgiveness.

B. We learn to put the focus on ourselves and to be good to ourselves.

C. We learn to detach with love; tough love.

D. We use the slogans: LET GO, LET GOD; EASY DOES IT; ONE DAY AT A TIME, etc.

E. We learn to feel our feelings, to accept and express them, and to build our self-esteem.

F. Through working the steps, we learn to accept the disease and to realize that our lives have become unmanageable and that we are powerless over the disease and that alcoholic. As we become willing to admit our defects and our sick thinking, we are able to change our attitudes and our reactions into actions. By working the program daily, admitting that we are powerless; we come to believe eventually in the spirituality of the program — that there is a solution other than ourselves, a Higher Power, God as we understand Him/She or by sharing our experiences, relating to others, welcoming newcomers, serving our group, we build our self-esteem.

PROGRESSION CHART
Alcohol Addiction

Read from left to right ⟶

EARLY STAGE

OCCASIONAL RELIEF DRINKING
CONSTANT RELIEF DRINKING
ONSET OF MEMORY BLACKOUTS
(IN SOME PERSONS)
INCREASE IN
ALCOHOL TOLERANCE
SNEAKING DRINKS
URGENCY OF FIRST DRINKS
INCREASING DEPENDENCE ON ALCOHOL
AVOID REFERENCE TO DRINKING
CONCERN/COMPLAINTS BY FAMILY
PREOCCUPATION WITH ALCOHOL
FEELINGS OF GUILT
DECREASE OF ABILITY TO STOP
DRINKING WHEN OTHERS DO
MEMORY BLACKOUTS INCREASE OR BEGIN
GRANDIOSE AND AGGRESSIVE
BEHAVIOR OR EXTRAVAGANCE
LOSS OF CONTROL
FAMILY MORE WORRIED, ANGRY
ALIBIS FOR DRINKING
GOES ON WAGON
PERSISTENT REMORSE
EFFORTS TO CONTROL FAIL REPEATEDLY
CHANGE OF PATTERN

MIDDLE STAGE

HIDES BOTTLES
TELEPHONISTS
PROMISES OR RESOLUTIONS FAIL
TRIES GEOGRAPHICAL ESCAPE
FAMILY AND FRIENDS AVOIDED
LOSS OF OTHER INTERESTS
WORK AND MONEY TROUBLES
FURTHER INCREASE IN MEMORY BLACKOUTS
TREMORS AND EARLY MORNING DRINKS
UNREASONABLE RESENTMENTS
PROTECTS SUPPLY
NEGLECT OF FOOD
DECREASE IN ALCOHOL TOLERANCE
PHYSICAL
ONSET OF LENGTHY INTOXICATIONS
DETERIORATION
DRINKING WITH INFERIORS
IMPAIRED
INDEFINABLE FEARS
THINKING
UNABLE TO INITIATE ACTION
OBSESSION WITH
VAGUE SPIRITUAL DESIRES
DRINKING
ALL ALIBIS EXHAUSTED
ETHICAL
COMPLETE DEFEAT ADMITTED
DETERIORATION

LATE STAGE

DENIAL

OBSESSIVE DRINKING CONTINUES
IN VICIOUS CIRCLES

THE ROAD TO RECOVERY

ENLIGHTENED AND INTERESTING WAY
OF LIFE OPENS UP WITH ROAD
AHEAD TO HIGHER LEVELS THAN
EVER BEFORE

FULL APPRECIATION OF
SPIRITUAL VALUES

GROUP THERAPY AND MUTUAL HELP CONTINUE

CONTENTMENT IN SOBRIETY

FIRST STEPS TOWARDS
ECONOMIC STABILITY

CONFIDENCE OF EMPLOYERS

APPRECIATION OF REAL VALUES

INCREASE OF EMOTIONAL CONTROL

REBIRTH OF IDEALS

FACTS FACED WITH COURAGE

NEW INTERESTS DEVELOP

NEW CIRCLE OF STABLE FRIENDS

ADJUSTMENTS TO FAMILY NEEDS

FAMILY AND FRIENDS
APPRECIATE EFFORTS

DESIRE TO ESCAPE GOES

RETURN OF SELF-ESTEEM

REALISTIC THINKING

DIMINISHING FEARS OF THE
UNKNOWN FUTURE

REGULAR NOURISHMENT TAKEN

APPRECIATION OF POSSIBILITIES
OF NEW WAY OF LIFE

CARE OF PERSONAL APPEARANCE

START OF GROUP THERAPY

ONSET OF NEW HOPE

GUILT REDUCTION

PHYSICAL OVERHAUL BY DOCTOR

SPIRITUAL NEEDS
EXAMINED

RIGHT THINKING BEGINS

STOPS TAKING
ALCOHOL

MEETS HAPPY SOBER ALCOHOLICS

TOLD ADDICTION CAN BE ARRESTED

LEARNS ALCOHOLISM IS AN ILLNESS
HONEST DESIRE FOR HELP

REHABILITATION

— Modified form M.M. Glatt

DO YOU HAVE THE DISEASE OF ALCOHOLISM?

When considering the possibility of alcoholism, please consider two things: First, the nature of the disease is to trick its victims into believing they can control their drinking. Second, making an effort to control one's drinking is, by itself, a sign of alcoholism. People who don't have an alcohol problem don't think twice about how much they drink. They set a limit and stick to it. If your drinking causes problems in any area of your life with your family, at work, in social settings, emotionally or physically, financially, or with the law, it's worth finding out more about this disease.

Alcoholism strikes one out of every ten people who drink. Not everyone has the physiological makeup to become alcoholic, but anyone who drinks could be at risk. Alcoholism doesn't discriminate. It affects people of all ethnic backgrounds, professions, and economic levels. It is not known precisely what causes this disease, but drinking is clearly a prerequisite. Therefore everyone who drinks should periodically evaluate their drinking patterns and behavior. This test, reproduced with permission of the National Council on Alcoholism, Inc. (NCA), will help you to determine whether or not you have symptoms of the disease. Answer the questions honestly, with a simple yes or no.

	Yes	No
1. Do you occasionally drink heavily after a disappointment, a quarrel, or when the boss gives you a hard time?	—	—
2. When you have trouble or feel under pressure, do you always drink more heavily than usual?	—	—

	Yes	No

3. Have you noticed that you are able to handle more alcohol than you did when you were first drinking? ___ ___

4. Did you ever wake up on the *"morning after"* and discover that you could not remember part of the evening before, even though your friends tell you that you did not *"pass out"*? ___ ___

5. When drinking with other people, do you try to have a few extra drinks when others will not know it? ___ ___

6. Are there certain occasions when you feel uncomfortable if alcohol is not available? ___ ___

7. Have you recently noticed that when you begin drinking you are in more of a hurry to get the first drink than you used to be? ___ ___

8. Do you sometimes feel a little guilty about your drinking? ___ ___

9. Are you secretly irritated when your family or friends discuss your drinking? ___ ___

10. Have you recently noticed an increase in the frequency of your memory *"blackouts"*? ___ ___

11. Do you often find that you wish to continue drinking after your friends say they have had enough? ___ ___

12. Do you usually have a reason for the occasions when you drink heavily? ___ ___

13. When you are sober, do you often regret things you have done or said while you were drinking? ___ ___

14. Have you tried switching brands or following different plans for controlling your drinking? ___ ___

	Yes	No

15. Have you often failed to keep the promises you have made to yourself about controlling or cutting down on your drinking? ___ ___

16. Have you ever tried to control your drinking by making a change in jobs or moving to a new location? ___ ___

17. Do you try to avoid family or close friends while you are drinking? ___ ___

18. Are you having an increasing number of financial and work problems? ___ ___

19. Do more people seem to be treating you unfairly without good reason? ___ ___

20. Do you eat very little or irregularly when you are drinking? ___ ___

21. Do you sometimes have the *"shakes"* in the morning and find that it helps to have a little drink? ___ ___

22. Have you recently noticed that you cannot drink as much as you once did? ___ ___

23. Do you sometimes stay drunk for several days at a time? ___ ___

24. Do you sometimes feel very depressed and wonder whether life is worth living? ___ ___

25. Sometimes after periods of drinking, do you see or hear things that are not there? ___ ___

26. Do you get terribly frightened after you have been drinking heavily? ___ ___

Any *"yes"* answer indicated a probable symptom of alcoholism. *"Yes"* answers to several of the questions indicate the following stages of alcoholism:

Questions 1 to 8: Early stage.
Questions 9 to 21: Middle stage.
Questions 22 to 26: Beginning of final stage.

Volunteers at local affiliate offices of NCA can provide further information to help you assess whether or not you have a drinking problem. They can also refer you to services and treatment programs in your area. Check the phone book under "Alcohol" or call **1-800-NCA-CALL** (1-800-622-2255) for the number of your community's NCA affiliate.

Books by Claudia Black

My Dad Loves Me, My Dad Has A Disease

It Will Never Happen To Me

Repeat After Me

It's Never Too Late To Have A Happy Childhood

Double Duty — Gay—Lesbian

Double Duty — Chemically Dependent

Double Duty — Food Addiction

Double Duty — Sexual Abuse

A complete catalogue of MAC products, including videotapes, note cards and related material, can be obtained free of charge from:

MAC PUBLISHING
a division of Claudja, inc.
5005 East 39th Avenue
Denver, CO 80207
(303) 331-0148 • Fax (303) 331-0212